Fundamentals of Ope

**Macmillan Computer Science Series**

*Consulting Editor*
Professor F. H. Sumner, University of Manchester

S. T. Allworth, *Introduction to Real-time Software Design*

Ian O. Angell, *A Practical Introduction to Computer Graphics*

G. M. Birtwistle, *Discrete Event Modelling on Simula*

T. B. Boffey, *Graph Theory in Operations Research*

Richard Bornat, *Understanding and Writing Compilers*

J. K. Buckle, *The ICL 2900 Series*

J. K. Buckle, *Software Configuration Management*

Robert Cole, *Computer Communications*

Derek Coleman, *A Structured Programming Approach to Data**

Andrew J. T. Colin, *Fundamentals of Computer Science*

Andrew J. T. Colin, *Programming and Problem-solving in Algol 68**

S. M. Deen, *Fundamentals of Data Base Systems**

J. B. Gosling, *Design of Arithmetic Units for Digital Computers*

David Hopkin and Barbara Moss, *Automata**

Roger Hutty, *Fortran for Students*

Roger Hutty, *Z80 Assembly Language Programming for Students*

H. Kopetz, *Software Reliability*

Graham Lee, *From Hardware to Software: an introduction to computers*

A. M. Lister, *Fundamentals of Operating Systems, second edition**

G. P. McKeown and V. J. Rayward-Smith, *Mathematics for Computing*

Brian Meek, *Fortran, PL/I and the Algols*

Derrick Morris and Roland N. Ibbett, *The MU5 Computer System*

John Race, *Case Studies in Systems Analysis*

B. S. Walker, *Understanding Microprocessors*

Peter J. L. Wallis, *Portable Programming*

I. R. Wilson and A. M. Addyman, *A Practical Introduction to Pascal*

---

* The titles marked with an asterisk were prepared during the Consulting Editorship of Professor
J. S. Rohl, University of Western Australia.

# Fundamentals of Operating Systems

A. M. Lister, M.A.

*University of Queensland*

## Second Edition

First edition 1975
Reprinted 1977, 1978
Second edition 1979
Reprinted 1980 (twice), 1981 (four times), 1982, 1983


*Published by*
THE MACMILLAN PRESS LTD
*London and Basingstoke*
*Companies and representatives*
*throughout the world*

*Typeset in Times Press Roman by*
*Styleset Limited, Salisbury, Wilts.*
*Printed in Hong Kong*

---

**British Library Cataloguing in Publication Data**

Lister, Andrew Martin
    Fundamentals of operating systems. —
    2nd ed.
    1. Operating systems (Computers)
    I. Title
    001.6'425       QA76.6

    ISBN 0–333–27287–0 Pbk

---

to my parents

# Contents

# *Preface*

An operating system is probably the most important part of the body of software which goes with any modern computer system. Its importance is reflected in the large amount of manpower usually invested in its construction, and in the mystique by which it is often surrounded. To the non-expert the design and construction of operating systems has often appeared an activity impenetrable to those who do not practise it. I hope this book will go some way toward dispelling the mystique, and encourage a greater general understanding of the principles on which operating systems are constructed.

The material in the book is based on a course of lectures I have given for the past few years to undergraduate students of computer science. The book is therefore a suitable introduction to operating systems for students who have a basic grounding in computer science, or for people who have worked with computers for some time. Ideally the reader should have a knowledge of programming and be familiar with general machine architecture, common data structures such as lists and trees, and the functions of system software such as compilers, loaders, and editors. It will also be helpful if he has had some experience of using a large operating system, seeing it, as it were, from the outside.

The first two chapters of the book define the functions of an operating system and describe some common operating system characteristics. Chapter 3 establishes the process as a basic concept in the discussion of the concurrent activities which go on inside an operating system, and describes how processes communicate with each other. The rest of the book then describes the construction of an operating system from the bottom up, starting at the interface with the machine hardware and ending at the interface with the user. By the end of the book the system which has been constructed is seen to possess the features demanded at the beginning.

Throughout the book I have tried to show how each stage in the construction of an operating system naturally follows on the previous ones, and have emphasised the logical structure of the system as a whole. I have done this for two reasons. The first is pedagogical: my experience indicates that students gain a better understanding of complex material if it is presented in a coherent manner. The second is frankly polemic: this is the way I believe operating systems should be built. Attention to structure and logical dependence are the best means we have of building operating systems which are easy to understand, easy to maintain, and relatively error free.

Finally, I would like to thank the many friends and colleagues who have helped in the writing of this book. In particular I would like to thank David Lyons, who has been a fertile source of ideas and comment; and David Howarth, who made valuable comments on an earlier draft. Thanks are also due to Colin Strutt, Morris Sloman, John Forecast, Ron Bushell and Bill Hart, who have made constructive suggestions for improving the text.

ANDREW LISTER

# Preface to the Second Edition

Any book on computer science suffers from the fact that its subject matter is undergoing rapid change, both technological and conceptual. A book on operating systems is no exception: the hardware on which systems run is being revolutionised by the large scale integration of components, and ideas about what operating systems should do are being modified by changing user requirements and expectations. Although this book is about 'fundamentals', which can be expected to be less volatile than other topics, it would be foolish to ignore the developments which have occurred in the four years since publication.

Consequently I have amended the text in three main ways for this edition. First, there is an additional chapter on reliability, a topic whose importance has increased dramatically as reliance on computer systems has grown in many areas of life. Secondly, the references to real-life operating systems have been updated to include systems which have come into use since the first edition, and references to the literature have been similarly updated. Thirdly, I have altered the presentation of certain topics so as better to reflect current ideas, and have expanded the conclusion to indicate what developments can be expected in the future.

Other changes in the text have been motivated by feedback from readers of the first edition. Here I owe a great debt to my students, who have had the perception to point out errors, and the good sense to expose inadequate exposition. Any improvements in this respect are due largely to them, though any remaining inadequacies are, of course, my own.

A.L.

# 1 *Introduction*

In this chapter and the next we attempt to answer the questions

> What is an operating system?
> What does it do?
> Why do we need one?

By answering these questions we hope to give the reader an idea of what we are trying to achieve when we discuss in later chapters how operating systems are constructed.

We start by examining the broad purpose of an operating system, and by classifying various types of operating system currently in existence.

Broadly speaking there are two design objectives in the construction of an operating system. The first is to transform a raw piece of hardware into a machine which is amenable to its potential users. This may be looked on as presenting the user with a *virtual machine*, whose characteristics are different from, but more tractable than, the underlying physical machine. For example, the input/output (I/O) capabilities of the basic hardware may be extremely complex and require sophisticated programming in order to utilise them; an operating system will relieve the user of the burden of understanding this complexity, and will present to him a virtual machine with much simpler to use, though equally powerful, I/O capabilities. The transformation of I/O capabilities is in fact a function of most operating systems.

The precise nature of the virtual machine will of course vary from application to application. For example, the characteristics of a computer required for an airline seat-reservation system will differ from those required for the control of scientific experiments. Clearly, the operating system design must be strongly influenced by the type of use for which the machine is intended. Unfortunately it is often the case with 'general-purpose machines' that the type of use cannot easily be identified; a common criticism of many manufacturers' systems is that in attempting to be all things to all men they wind up being totally satisfactory to no one.

The second design objective in operating system construction is to give good value for money, that is to make the best possible use of the hardware available. One might speculate as to whether the motivation for this is aesthetic, or simply a variation on the profit motive! Certainly the economic argument is compelling:

it is pointless to produce a system with all the 'bells and whistles' if the cost, either in capital outlay or in operating efficiency, is prohibitive.

It is useful in discussing the broad functions of an operating system to divide the areas of application into *real-time* and *job-shop*. By a real-time system we mean one in which a response must be given to an external stimulus within a limited period of time. For example, in an airline seat-reservation system a request for a seat booking must be answered during the few minutes that the customer is prepared to wait. Similarly, in a system for the automatic control of an oil refinery, a response must be given to an increase in pressure within the space of time determined by safety. A job-shop system, on the other hand, is one which processes a sequence of jobs (tasks) with no particular time constraints, except those of overall throughput. Such a system might be employed to process the salaries, orders and sales in a marketing organisation, or to run a variety of problem-solving programs for university research groups or students.

We can examine typical systems of each type and discuss the functions we expect of them.

## 1.1 REAL-TIME SYSTEMS

### (1) Process Control

The term process control generally implies the control by computer of an industrial process, such as the refining of oil or the manufacture of machine tools. It can be extended to include such things as environmental control in a space capsule or the monitoring of a patient's condition in a hospital. The common feature of all these applications is *feedback*; that is, the computer receives input from the controlled process, computes a response which will maintain its stability, and initiates the mechanism for giving it. If the input, for example, signifies a dangerous rise in temperature, then the response may well be to open a valve to increase the flow of coolant. Clearly there is a critical time in which the response must be given if the process is to remain in equilibrium, let alone safe! The main function of the operating system in process control is to provide maximum reliability with the minimum of operator intervention, and to 'fail safe' in the event of any hardware malfunctions.

### (2) File Interrogation Systems

The distinguishing feature of these systems is a large set of data, or *data base*, which can be interrogated for information. The response to information requests must occur within a short time (typically less than a minute), and the data base must be capable of being modified as information is updated. Examples are management information systems, where the data base consists of information on company performance, and medical information systems, in which the data base is a set of patients' records. The user (company manager or doctor) expects to be able to access information without any knowledge of how the data base is organised, either in terms of software structure or hardware storage devices. Hence the operating system must make interrogation facilities available without involving the user in details of implementation.

### (3) Transaction Processing

Transaction processing systems are characterised by a data base which is frequently being modified, perhaps several times a second. Typical applications are in airline seat-reservations and banking. In the former the data base contains information on seat availability, and is modified each time a seat is booked; in the latter it consists of details of accounts, which are updated for every credit and debit. The real-time character of transaction processing derives from the necessity of keeping the data base up to date; clearly the system is useless if transactions are made on incorrect data. Further problems arise in dealing with simultaneous transactions on the same piece of data (for example two travel agents trying to book the same seat). The individual user should of course be unaware of these problems, and the operating system must resolve them so that he has the impression of being the sole user of the system.

### 1.2 JOB-SHOP SYSTEMS

Job-shop systems are designed to handle a continuous flow of work in the form of jobs to be run on the computer. Each job performs a specific task for a particular user (for example, analysis of survey data, solution of differential equations, calculation of monthly payroll) and typically consists of running one or more programs. In a simple case, say that of survey analysis, the job may be no more than the running of an already compiled program with a particular set of data. More complicated jobs may involve modifying a program by use of an editor, compiling it, and finally running it. Because of the variety of jobs which may be submitted, the system must be able to support a large number of utilities such as compilers for various languages, assemblers, editors, debugging packages, and a file system for long-term storage of information. It must also be able to handle the wide variety of peripherals which may be required (for example, card reader and punch, paper tape reader and punch, line printer, magnetic tapes and discs, graph plotter). The provision and control of these facilities, together with the organisation of the flow of work, are the broad functions of a job-shop operating system.

Job-shop systems can be classified into two groups: (1) *batch*, and (2) *multi-access*. The chief characteristic of a batch system is that once a job enters the computer the user has no further contact with it until it has been completed. A typical job is punched on cards or paper tape and passed to an operator for submission to the machine. When the job is complete the operator dispatches the output back to the user. In most cases the job is submitted to the computer

through input and output devices within the computer room itself; however
some batch systems, called *remote job entry* (RJE) systems allow submission of
jobs through I/O devices which may be at some distance from the central installation and connected to it by a data transmission line. An RJE system may support
several outlying I/O stations, and must of course return output to the station
at which a job was submitted. In neither a straightforward batch system nor an
RJE system is there any opportunity for a user to interact with his job while
it is running.

In a multi-access system, on the other hand, a user may submit a job by
typing on a terminal and may use the terminal to monitor and control the job
as it runs. He may for example correct the syntax errors reported by a compiler,
or supply data which is dependent on the results so far received. The operating
system shares the computing resources among the different jobs so that it
appears to each user that he has the entire machine to himself. Multi-access
systems straddle the dividing line between job-shop and real-time in that responses
to user actions must be given within a limited period of time if the user is to be
satisfied. The distinction is that failure to meet desired response time in a multi-
access system results in nothing worse than irritation and impatience, whereas
in a true real-time system it may well be catastrophic.

Both job-shop and real-time systems may be implemented on either a single
computer, or on a number of connected computers. In the latter case the
separate computers may share the workload equally between them, or each
computer may be dedicated to servicing only one particular aspect of it. For
example, one computer may be devoted to handling all I/O from remote
stations, while another performs all work requiring intensive numeric processing.
The computers may be located in the same room, possibly sharing memory and
backing store, or they may be located at some distance from each other and
communicate by means of data transmission lines. In such *distributed systems*
the operating system must coordinate the activities of each computer, and
ensure that the appropriate information flows between them as required.


## 1.3 THE 'PAPER' OPERATING SYSTEM

The majority of this book will be devoted to job-shop systems. However,
several of the problems discussed also arise in other systems, and we shall indicate the relevance of our discussion to other systems wherever appropriate.

In order to study the way in which a job-shop system is constructed we shall
build a 'paper' operating system; that is, we shall develop a hypothetical system
on paper, in the hope that this will illustrate the principles involved. It will be
our aim to develop this system in a logical manner, in that each stage of
development will follow naturally from the previous one. The final structure
will in some ways resemble an onion, in which each layer provides a set of
functions which are dependent only on the layers within it. The direction of
construction will be from the inside outwards, or 'bottom up', so that starting

from a nucleus we shall add layers for memory management, I/O handling, file access, and so on.

It must be admitted that very few real-life operating systems actually exhibit the neatly layered structure suggested; notable exceptions are T.H.E. (Dijkstra, 1968), RC-4000 (Hansen, 1970), UNIX (Ritchie and Thompson, 1974), and, in the commercial world, VME/B for the ICL 2900 series (Keedy, 1976; Huxtable and Pinkerton, 1977). Indeed it can fairly be said that many existing systems display very little logical structure at all. This sad fact may be attributed to three factors: first, most current systems were designed at a time when the principles of operating system construction were far less clear than they are now; second, the common technique of using large numbers of people to write complex software seldom results in a 'clean' product; and third, the previously mentioned desire for a system to be all things to all men often leads to the *ad hoc* . attachment of new features long after the initial design stage. It is also the case that constraints imposed by peculiarities of hardware may often cause a well structured design to become blurred in implementation. However, we can reasonably hope that these constraints will become fewer as hardware design is modified to meet the needs of operating system construction.

As the development of our paper operating system proceeds we shall compare it with existing systems, and relate the techniques we use to those employed elsewhere. In this way we shall keep our operating system firmly rooted in current practice, while using it as a vehicle for conveying the principles of operating system construction.

# 2 Functions and Characteristics of an Operating System

In this chapter we discuss in more detail the functions which we expect a job-shop operating system to fulfil, and isolate some of the characteristics it must exhibit in order to do so.

## 2.1 OPERATING SYSTEM FUNCTIONS

We take as our starting point the raw machine — the basic computer hardware consisting of central processor, memory, and various peripherals. (We defer until later consideration of computers with more than one central processor.) In the absence of any software aids, the operation of loading and running a user program must be performed entirely under human control. The operator must perform a tedious sequence of tasks something like this

(1)  place the source program cards in the card reader
(2)  initiate a program to read in the cards
(3)  initiate a compiler to compile the source program
(4)  place the data cards, if any, in the card reader
(5)  initiate execution of the compiled program
(6)  remove results from the line printer

The speed of the machine is obviously dependent on the rate at which the operator can press buttons and feed peripherals, and the system is therefore very much operator-limited.

An obvious first improvement is to make the machine carry out automatically, without operator intervention, the sequence of steps necessary to read-in, compile, load and execute programs. The operator's role is thus reduced to loading cards at one end of the machine and tearing off paper at the other, and throughput is consequently increased. Of course one rarely gets something for nothing, and the price paid for increased speed is the dedication of part of the machine to a program which can perform the necessary job sequencing operations. Since all jobs do not require the same sequencing operations (some jobs, for example, may not need compilation) the control program must be able to infer from one or more control cards precisely what operations are to be performed in any particular case. In other words the control program must be capable of interpreting a *job control language*. Furthermore, the errors which will inevitably occur in some jobs cannot be allowed to affect jobs later in the sequence, and so the control program must be responsible for handling errors in some rational fashion. A control program with these features is in fact an embryonic operating system.

A system of this type is clearly limited by the speed at which it can perform I/O, and the next stage in improving efficiency is to reduce the I/O dependency. Historically, this was first achieved by the technique of *off-lining*, whereby all output and input was performed to and from magnetic tape. The task of converting card (or paper tape) input to magnetic tape, and magnetic tape output to line printer or punch, was relegated to a satellite computer of less power and cost. The transfer of magnetic tapes between satellite and main computer was by hand. Off-lining systems, notably the IBM Fortran Monitor System, ran successfully from the late 1950s into the mid 1960s.

Off-lining reduced I/O dependency by ensuring that all I/O was performed on magnetic tape, which was at the time the fastest cheaply available medium. The price paid was the addition to the embryonic operating system of a set of routines for coding and packing on magnetic tape data eventually destined for some other peripheral (and conversely for input). It should also be noted that because magnetic tape is essentially a serial medium there was no notion of scheduling jobs to run in any order other than that in which they were presented.

In order to eliminate I/O dependency rather than merely reduce it, techniques must be employed whereby I/O can be overlapped with processing. This is possible with the aid of two hardware devices — the *channel* and the *interrupt*. A channel is a device which controls one or more peripherals, performing data transfers between the peripherals and memory quite independently of the central processor. An interrupt is a signal which transfers control of the central processor to a fixed location, while at the same time storing the previous value of the program counter. Thus the program being executed at the time of the interrupt is temporarily abandoned but can be resumed later (that is, it is *interrupted*). An interrupt from a channel acts as a signal to indicate that a data transfer has been completed. Hence it is possible for the central processor to initiate a peripheral transfer, to continue processing while the channel controls the transfer, and to receive notification by means of an interrupt when the transfer is complete. (The reader who wishes to learn more about channels and interrupt hardware is referred to any text on computer architecture, such as Foster, 1970, or Stone, 1975.)

It now becomes possible to read-in jobs on to some suitable storage medium, usually disc or drum, and to execute them one by one at the same time as other jobs are being read-in. The additions to our rapidly growing operating system are a routine to handle the interrupts and a routine to decide which of the several jobs on disc to run next. This latter function, that of *scheduling*, derives from the use as input medium of disc or drum, which are random access devices, rather than magnetic tape, which is serial. A system working in this way is known as a *single stream batch monitor*. (Single stream means only one job is executed at a time.) Such systems were predominant in the mid 1960s.

The main disadvantage of a single stream system is the dedication of the entire machine to the execution of a single job, no matter how large or small. This disadvantage can be overcome by *multiprogramming* — the running of several programs in the same machine at the same time. The idea is that several programs are held simultaneously in memory, and the central processor divides its time between them according to the resources (such as channels or peripherals) that each one needs at any instant. In this way it is possible, by having a suitable mix of jobs in the machine at any time, to achieve optimal utilisation of resources. This includes central processor utilisation, as whenever a job is waiting for an I/O transfer to be completed the processor can switch to some other job currently in the machine. The additional load on the operating system is the control of resources and the protection of one job from the activities of another. An operating system of this type is called a *multi-stream batch monitor*, and versions abounded on all large computers of early 1970s (for example GEORGE 3 on the ICL 1900 series, and OS/360 on the IBM 360 and 370 series). The development of these systems owed much to the pioneering work done in the early 1960s on the Atlas computer at Manchester University.

At this stage of our progression from the raw machine we have quite a sophisticated system which is making good use of the hardware available. Its main disadvantage from the user's point of view is the lack of any interaction with his job as it passes through the computer. Interaction is valuable in many situations, particularly during the development and debugging of a program. For example, debugging becomes easier if the programmer is immediately able to test modifications and see their effect, making further modifications as necessary. Similarly, many problem-solving programs require 'steering' by the user, that is, the user directs the further action of the program after examining the results so far. In order for interaction to be feasible, the multi-stream batch system must be modified to accept input from users typing at remote terminals; in other words it must become a multi-access system as described in the previous chapter. In the early 1970s most manufacturers produced multi-access operating systems for their larger computers; examples were MINIMOP (ICL 1900), TSS/360 (IBM 360 and 370), and TOPS-10 (DEC System-10). More recently the batch and multi-access modes of operation have been combined in such systems as MVS (IBM 370), MCP (Burroughs 6700 and 7700), and VME/B (ICL 2900).

The foregoing discussion has led us to an operating system which must perform at least the following functions

(1)   Job sequencing
(2)   Job control language interpretation
(3)   Error handling
(4)   I/O handling
(5)   Interrupt handling
(6)   Scheduling
(7)   Resource control
(8)   Protection
(9)   Multi-access

Additionally, the operating system should be easy to run from the operator's point of view, and easy to control from the installation manager's point of view. We can therefore add the further functions

(10)  Provision of good interface to the operator
(11)  Accounting of computing resources

It will be clear from this that operating systems are decidely non-trivial animals, and it is not surprising that an enormous amount of effort has been spent in writing them. As a step towards a coherent structure for an operating system we can abstract from the above list of functions certain characteristics which the system must exhibit. These, together with the attendant problems in displaying them, are listed in the following section.

## 2.2 OPERATING SYSTEM CHARACTERISTICS

### (1) Concurrency

Concurrency is the existence of several simultaneous, or parallel, activities. Examples are the overlapping of I/O operations with computation, and the coexistence in memory of several user programs. Concurrency raises problems of switching from one activity to another, of protecting one activity against the effects of another, and synchronising activities which are mutually dependent.

### (2) Sharing

Concurrent activities may be required to share resources or information. The motivation for this is fourfold.

(a)  Cost: it is extravagant to provide sufficient resources for all users separately.
(b)  Building on the work of others: it is useful to be able to use other people's programs or routines.
(c)  Sharing data: it may be necessary to use the same data base for several different programs, possibly working for several different users.
(d)  Removing redundancy: it is economical to share a single copy of a program (for example a compiler) between several users, rather than provide a separate copy for each user.

Problems associated with sharing are resource allocation, simultaneous access to data, simultaneous execution of programs, and protection against corruption.

### (3) Long-term Storage

The need for sharing programs and data implies the need for long-term storage of information. Long-term storage also allows a user the convenience of keeping his programs or data in the computer rather than on some external medium (for example, cards). The problems arising are those of providing easy access, protection against interference (malicious or otherwise), and protection against system failure.

### (4) Nondeterminacy

An operating system must be *determinate* in the sense that the same program run today or tomorrow with the same data should produce the same results. On the other hand it is *indeterminate* in that it must respond to events which will occur in an unpredictable order. These events are such things as resource requests, run-time errors in programs, and interrupts from peripheral devices. Because of the enormous number of contingencies which can arise it is clearly unreasonable to expect to write the operating system to cater for them all individually. Instead the system must be written so as to handle *any* sequence of events.

It is worth pointing out that none of these characteristics are peculiar to job-shop systems alone. Long-term storage, for example, is clearly required in file interrogation systems, and concurrency is a prime feature of transaction processing systems.

To conclude this chapter we mention briefly a few features which it is desirable for a job-shop operating system to display.

### 2.3 DESIRABLE FEATURES

### (1) Efficiency

The need for efficiency has already been alluded to. Unfortunately, it is difficult to light on one single criterion by which the efficiency of an operating system can be judged: various possible criteria are listed below.

(a)   mean time between jobs
(b)   unused central processor time
(c)   turn-round time for batch jobs
(d)   response time (in multi-access systems)
(e)   resource utilisation
(f)   throughput (jobs per hour)

Not all these criteria can be satisfied simultaneously; we shall have more to say in later chapters about design decisions which effectively give more weight to some than to others.

### (2) Reliability

Ideally an operating system should be completely error-free, and be able to handle all contingencies. In practice this is never the case, but we shall see in chapter 10 how considerable progress can be made towards this goal.

## (3) Maintainability

It should be possible to maintain an operating system — enhancing it or correcting errors — without employing an army of systems programmers. This implies that the system should be modular in construction, with clearly defined interfaces between the modules, and that it should be well documented.

## (4) Small Size

Space used to hold the operating system, whether in memory or on backing store, is wasted as far as productive computing is concerned. Furthermore, a large system is liable to be more prone to error, and take longer to write, than a small one.

To summarise what has been done in this chapter: we have discussed the general functions we expect a job-shop operating system to fulfil; we have isolated some crucial operating system characteristics; and we have enumerated some desirable system features. In the next chapter we shall examine some basic tools which will help us construct the system we require.

# 3 Concurrent Processes

Before we can start a detailed study of operating systems, we need to introduce some basic concepts and develop a few tools. This will be the purpose of the present chapter.

## 3.1 PROGRAMS, PROCESSES AND PROCESSORS

We start by considering an operating system as a set of activities, each providing one of the functions, such as scheduling or I/O handling, described in chapter 2. Each activity consists of the execution of one or more programs, and will be invoked whenever the corresponding function is to be provided. We use the word *process* to describe an activity of this kind. (Other names in the literature are *task* and *computation*.) A process may thus be thought of as a sequence of actions, performed by executing a sequence of instructions (a program), whose net result is the provision of some system function. We can extend the concept to include the provision of user functions as well as system functions, so that the execution of a user program is also called a process.

A process may involve the execution of more than one program; conversely, a single program or routine may be involved in more than one process. For example, a routine for adding an item to a list might be used by any process engaged in queue manipulation. Hence the knowledge that a particular program is currently being executed does not tell us much about what activity is being pursued or what function is being implemented. It is largely for this reason that the concept of a process is more useful than that of a program when talking about operating systems.

A process is able to proceed by virtue of an agent which executes the associated program. This agent is known as a *processor*. We say that a processor *runs* a process, or that a process *runs on* a processor. A processor is something which executes instructions; depending on the nature of the instructions the processor may be implemented in hardware alone, or in a combination of both hardware and software. For example, a central processing unit (CPU) is a processor for executing machine language instructions, while a CPU together with a BASIC interpreter can form a processor for executing BASIC instructions. The transformation, discussed in chapter 1, of a raw computer into a virtual machine may in fact be regarded as the combination of the computer hardware and the operating system to provide a processor capable of running user processes (that is, a processor capable of executing user instructions).

The program or programs associated with a process need not be implemented as software. The action of a channel, for example, in performing a data transfer, may be looked on as a process in which the associated program is wired into the channel hardware. Viewed in this way the channel, or indeed any peripheral device, is a processor which is capable of executing only a single process.

The concepts of process and processor can readily be used to interpret both concurrency and nondeterminacy, which were two of the operating system characteristics outlined in the last chapter.

Concurrency can be regarded as the activation of several processes (that is, the execution of several programs) at the same time. Provided there are as many processors as processes this presents no logical difficulty. If, as is more usual, there are fewer processors than processes then apparent concurrency can be obtained by switching processors from one process to another. If the switching is done at suitably small intervals of time then the system will give the illusion of concurrency when viewed on a longer time scale. Apparent concurrency is in effect achieved by interleaving processes on a single processor.

It may be helpful at this point to draw an analogy with the activities of a secretary in a general office. Each of the jobs a secretary has to perform, such as typing letters, filing invoices, or taking dictation, can be likened to a process in an operating system. The processor is the secretary herself, and the sequence of instructions which defines each job is analogous to a program. If the office is busy then the secretary may have to break off one job to do another, and in this situation she would probably complain of 'doing several jobs at the same time'. Of course she is only doing one job at once, but the frequent switching from one activity to another gives an overall impression of concurrency. We may pursue the analogy further by observing that before the secretary can change to another activity she must make sufficient note of what she is currently doing in order to pick up the thread again later. Similarly, a processor in a computing system must record information about the process it is currently running before it can switch to some other process. The precise nature of the information to be stored will be discussed in the next chapter; for the moment we remark only that it must be sufficient to enable the process to be resumed at some later time.

Carrying the analogy still further, we can introduce additional secretaries (processors) into the office. True concurrency can now exist between the various secretaries performing different tasks, though apparent concurrency may still persist as each secretary switches from one task to another and back again. Only when the number of secretaries is equal to the number of jobs to be done can all the jobs be performed in a truly concurrent manner. The analogue of the processor, such as an I/O device, which can perform only a single process, is the junior secretary who is capable only of making the tea.

Bearing in mind the foregoing discussion, we define *concurrent processing* (or *parallel processing*) to mean that if a snapshot is taken of the system as a whole then several processes may be found somewhere between their starting points and their end points. This definition clearly includes both true and apparent concurrency.

Nondeterminacy is the second operating system characteristic which can easily be described in terms of processes. If we regard processes as sequences of actions which can be interrupted between steps, then nondeterminacy is reflected in the unpredictable order in which the interruptions may occur, and hence the unpredictable order in which the sequences proceed. Reverting to our secretarial analogy, we can liken the unpredictable events which occur in an operating system to telephones ringing in an office. It cannot be known in advance when a particular telephone will ring, how long it will take to deal with the call, or what effect the call will have on the various jobs being done in the office. We can observe, however, that the secretary who answers the telephone must note what she is currently doing so that she can return to it later. Similarly, the interruption of a process must be accompanied by the recording of information which will subsequently enable the process to be resumed. The information recorded is the same as that required when processors switch among processes in order to achieve concurrency. Indeed, interruption of a process can be regarded as a switch, caused by some unpredictable event, of a processor away from the process.

We can summarise what has been said so far as follows. A process is a sequence of actions, and is therefore dynamic, whereas a program is a sequence of instructions, and is therefore static. A processor is an agent for running a process. Nondeterminacy and concurrency can be described in terms of interrupting processes between actions and of switching processors among processes. In order to effect interruption and switching sufficient information about a process must be stored in order that it may later be resumed.

## 3.2 COMMUNICATION BETWEEN PROCESSES

The processes within a computing system do not of course act in isolation. On the one hand they must co-operate to achieve the desired objective of running user jobs; on the other hand they are in competition for the use of limited resources such as processors, memory, or files. The two elements of co-operation and competition imply the need for some form of communication between processes. The areas in which communication is essential may be categorised as follows.

### (1) Mutual Exclusion

System resources may be classified as *shareable*, meaning that they may be used by several processes concurrently (in the sense defined in the previous section), or *non-shareable*, meaning that their use is restricted to one process at a time. The non-shareability of a resource derives from one of two reasons.

(a)     The physical nature of the resource makes it impracticable for it to be shared. A typical example is a paper tape reader, where it is impracticable to switch tapes between successive characters.

(b)     The resource is such that if it were used by several processes concurrently the actions of one process could interfere with those of another. A particularly common example is a memory location which contains a variable accessible to more than one process: if one process tests the variable while another modifies it then the result will be unpredictable and usually disastrous. For instance, suppose that in an airline booking system the availability of a particular seat is represented by the contents of a certain location in memory. Then if the location were accessible to more than one process at a time it would be possible for two travel agents to reserve the seat simultaneously by following the unfortunate sequence of actions below.

Agent A sees the seat is free
and consults his client

                                      Agent B sees the seat is free
                                      and consults his client

Agent A reserves the seat

                                      Agent B reserves the seat

Non-shareable resources therefore include most peripherals, writeable files, and data areas which are subject to modification; shareable resources include CPUs, read-only files, and areas of memory which contain pure procedures or data protected against modification.

The mutual exclusion problem is that of ensuring that non-shareable resources are accessed by only one process at a time.

## (2) Synchronisation

Generally speaking the speed of one process relative to another is unpredictable, since it depends on the frequency of interruption of each process and on how often and for how long each process is granted a processor. We say that processes run *asynchronously* with respect to each other. However, to achieve successful co-operation there are certain points at which processes must synchronise their activities. These are points beyond which a process cannot proceed until another process has completed some activity. For example, a process which schedules user jobs cannot proceed until an input process has read at least one job into the machine. Similarly, a computational process producing output may not be able to proceed until its previous output has been printed. It is the operating system's responsibility to provide mechanisms by which synchronisation can be effected.

## (3) Deadlock

When several processes compete for resources it is possible for a situation to arise in which no process can continue because the resources each one requires are held by another. This situation is called *deadlock*, or *deadly embrace*. It is analogous to the traffic jam which occurs when two opposing streams of traffic, in trying to turn across each other's path, become completely immobilised because each stream occupies the road space needed by the other. The avoidance of deadlock, or the limitation of its effects, is clearly one of the functions of the operating system.

## 3.3 SEMAPHORES

The most important single contribution towards inter-process communication was the introduction (Dijkstra, 1965) of the concept of *semaphores* and the primitive operations *wait* and *signal* which act on them. (*Wait and signal are* often referred to by Dijkstra's original names P and V which are the initial letters of the corresponding Dutch words. We shall, however, adopt the more recent and descriptive terminology.)

A semaphore is a non-negative integer which, apart from initialisation of its value, can be acted upon only by the operations *wait* and *signal*. These operations act only on semaphores, and their effect is defined as follows.

### *signal(s)*

The effect is to increase the value of the semaphore $s$ by one, the increase being regarded as an indivisible operation. Indivisibility implies that *signal(s)* is not equivalent to the assignment statement '$s: = s + 1$'. For suppose that two processes A and B both wish to perform the operation '*signal* (s)' when the value of $s$ is, say, 3. Then the value of $s$ when both operations are complete will be 5. Suppose on the other hand that in similar circumstances both processes wish to execute '$s: = s + 1$'. Then A could evaluate the expression $s + 1$, finding it equal to 4; before A can assign the result to $s$, B also evaluates $s + 1$ with the same result. Each process then assigns the value 4 to $s$, and one of the desired increments is lost.

### *wait(s)*

The effect is to decrease the value of the semaphore $s$ by 1 as soon as the result would be non-negative. Again the operation is indivisible. The *wait* operation implies a potential delay, for when it acts on a semaphore whose value is 0, the process executing the operation can proceed only when some other process has increased the value of the semaphore to 1 by a *signal* operation. The indivisibility of the operation means that if several processes are delayed then only one of them can successfully complete the operation when the semaphore becomes positive. No assumption is made about which process this is.

The effects of the wait and signal operations may be summarised as

$wait(s)$ : **when** $s > 0$ **do** decrement $s$
$signal(s)$ : increment $s$

where $s$ is any semaphore.

It can be seen from these definitions that every *signal* operation on a semaphore increases its value by 1 and every successful (that is, completed) *wait* operation decreases its value by 1. Hence the value of a semaphore is related to the number of *wait* and *signal* operations on it by the relation

$$val\ (sem) = C\ (sem) + ns\ (sem) - nw\ (sem) \tag{3.1}$$

where

$val\ (sem)$     is the value of semaphore *sem*
$C\ (sem)$       is its initial value
$ns\ (sem)$      is the number of *signal* operations on it
$nw\ (sem)$      is the number of successful *wait* operations on it

But, by definition

$$val\ (sem) \geqslant 0$$

Hence we derive the important relation

$$nw\ (sem) \leqslant ns\ (sem) + C\ (sem) \tag{3.2}$$

in which equality holds if and only if $val\ (sem) = 0$.

The relation 3.2 is invariant under *wait* and *signal* operations; that is, it is true however many operations are performed.

The implementation of semaphores and of the *wait* and *signal* operations will be discussed in the next chapter. For the present we shall take their implementability for granted, and use them to solve the problems listed earlier.


## (1) Mutual Exclusion

Non-shareable resources, whether peripherals, files, or data in memory, can be protected from simultaneous access by several processes by preventing the processes from concurrently executing the pieces of program through which access is made. These pieces of program are called *critical sections*, and mutual exclusion in the use of resources can be regarded as mutual exclusion in the execution of critical sections. For example, processes may be mutually excluded from accessing a table of data if all the routines which read or update the table are written as critical sections such that only one may be executed at once.

Exclusion can be achieved by the simple expedient of enclosing each critical section by *wait* and *signal* operations on a single semaphore whose initial value is 1. Thus each critical section is programmed as

> *wait* (*mutex*);
>
> > critical section
>
> *signal* (*mutex*);

where *mutex* is the name of a semaphore.

The reader will see by inspection that if the initial value of *mutex* is 1 then mutual exclusion is indeed assured, since at most one process can execute *wait* (*mutex*) before another executes *signal* (*mutex*). More formally, application of relation 3.2 gives

$$nw \ (mutex) \leqslant ns \ (mutex) + 1$$

which implies that at most one process can be inside its critical section at any time.

Furthermore, a process is never unnecessarily prevented from entering its critical section; entry is prevented only if some other process is already inside its own critical section. We can see this by observing that a process is denied entry only if the value of *mutex* is 0. In this case relation 3.2 indicates that

$$nw \ (mutex) = ns \ (mutex) + 1$$

In other words the number of successful *wait* operations on *mutex* exceeds the number of signal operations by 1, which implies that some process is within its critical section.

Our conclusion is that each time a process wishes to access a shared variable or a shared resource then it must effect the access via a critical section which is protected by a semaphore as above.

As an example suppose that an operating system contains two processes *A* and *B* which respectively add items to and remove items from a queue. In order that the queue pointers do not become confused it may be necessary to restrict access to the queue to only one process at a time. Thus the addition and removal of items would be coded as critical sections as below.

| *Program for Process A* | *Program for Process B* |
|---|---|
| . | . |
| . | . |
| . | . |
| *wait* (*mutex*); | *wait* (*mutex*); |
|     add item to queue |     remove item from queue |
| *signal (mutex);* | *signal (mutex);* |
| . | . |
| . | . |
| . | . |

At this point the suspicious reader may wonder whether the mutual exclusion problem could have been solved without the additional formalism of semaphores and their associated operations. On the face of it this suspicion might appear well founded, for it seems possible to derive a solution by protecting each critical section by a single simple variable (called *gate*, say). When *gate* is set to *open* (represented by the value 1, say), entry to the critical section is allowed; when it is set to *closed* (represented by 0), entry is not allowed. Thus a critical section would be coded as

**while** *gate* = *closed* **do** null operation;

*gate* := *closed*;

     critical section

*gate* := *open*;

Thus each process entering the critical section tests that *gate* is *open* (and loops until it is); it then sets *gate* to *closed*, preventing other processes entering the section. On exit, the process resets *gate* to *open*, freeing the section for execution by another process.

Unfortunately this simple solution will not work. The reason lies in the separation of the test for an open gate in line 1 from the closing of the gate in line 2. As a consequence of this separation two processes executing in parallel may each find an open gate at line 1 before either has the chance to close it at line 2. The result is that both processes enter the critical section together.

Semaphores avoid a similar difficulty by the insistence that the *wait* and *signal* operations are indivisible; there is no possibility of two processes acting on the same semaphore at the same time. The implementation of semaphores, to be discussed in chapter 4, must of course ensure that this is so.

## (2) Synchronisation

The simplest form of synchronisation is that a process *A* should not proceed beyond a point L1 until some other process *B* has reached L2. Examples of this situation arise whenever *A* requires information at point L1 which is provided by *B* when it reaches L2. The synchronisation can be programmed as follows

| *Program for Process A* | *Program for Process B* |
|---|---|
| . | . |
| . | . |
| . | . |
| L1 : *wait* (*proceed*); | L2 : *signal* (*proceed*); |
| . | . |
| . | . |
| . | . |

where *proceed* is a semaphore with initial value 0.

It is clear from the above programs that $A$ cannot proceed beyond L1 until $B$ has executed the signal operation at L2. (Of course if $B$ executes the signal operation before $A$ reaches L1 then $A$ is not delayed at all.) Again we can use relation 3.2 to demonstrate this more formally; we have

$$nw\ (proceed) \leqslant ns\ (proceed)$$

which implies that $A$ cannot pass L1 before $B$ passes L2.

The above example is asymmetric in that the progress of $A$ is regulated by that of $B$ but not vice versa. The case in which two processes each regulate the progress of the other is exemplified by the classic problem of the producer and consumer. Since this problem is typical of many which arise in inter-process communication we shall describe it in some detail.

A set of 'producer' processes and a set of 'consumer' processes communicate by means of a buffer into which the producers deposit items and from which the consumers extract them. The producers continually repeat the cycle 'produce item – deposit item in buffer', and the consumers repeat a similar cycle 'extract item from buffer – consume item'. A typical producer might be a computational process placing lines of ouput in a buffer, while the corresponding consumer might be the process which prints each line. The buffer is of limited capacity, being large enough to hold $N$ items of equal size. The synchronisation required is twofold: firstly, the producers cannot put items into the buffer if it is already full, and secondly, the consumers cannot extract items if the buffer is empty. In other words, if the number of items deposited is $d$, and the number of items extracted is $e$, we must ensure that

$$0 \leqslant d - e \leqslant N \tag{3.3}$$

Furthermore, the buffer must be protected from simultaneous access by several processes, lest the actions of one (for example in updating pointers) disturb the actions of another. Hence both the deposition and extraction of items must be coded as critical sections.

We postulate the following solution to the problem

| *Program for producers* | *Program for consumers* |
|---|---|

```
repeat indefinitely              repeat indefinitely
begin                            begin
      produce item;                    wait(item available);
      wait(space available);           wait(buffer
      wait(buffer                        manipulation);
        manipulation);                 extract item from buffer;
        deposit item in buffer;      signal(buffer
      signal(buffer                    manipulation);
        manipulation);               signal(space available);
        signal(item available)       consume item
end                              end
```

Synchronisation is achieved through the semaphores *space available* and *item available* whose initial values are $N$ and $0$ respectively. Mutual exclusion of processes from accessing the buffer is effected by the semaphore *buffer manipulation* with initial value 1.

We must now show that this solution satisfies relation 3.3. If we apply the invariance relation 3.2. to the two synchronisation semaphores we obtain

$$nw \ (space \ available) \leqslant ns \ (space \ available) + N \qquad (3.4)$$

and

$$nw \ (item \ available) \leqslant ns \ (item \ available) \qquad (3.5)$$

But we observe from the order of operations in the program for the producers that

$$ns \ (item \ available) \leqslant d \leqslant nw \ (space \ available) \qquad (3.6)$$

and from the order of operations in the program for the consumers that

$$ns \ (space \ available) \leqslant e \leqslant nw \ (item \ available) \qquad (3.7)$$

Hence, from relation 3.6

$$d \leqslant nw \ (space \ available)$$
$$\leqslant ns \ (space \ available) + N \qquad \text{by 3.4}$$
$$\leqslant e + N \qquad \text{by 3.7}$$

Similarly, from relation 3.7

$$e \leqslant nw \ (item \ available)$$
$$\leqslant ns \ (item \ available) \qquad \text{by 3.5}$$
$$\leqslant d \qquad \text{by 3.6}$$

Combination of these two results gives

$$e \leqslant d \leqslant e + N$$

which shows that relation 3.3 is satisfied as required.


The solution to the producer–consumer problem can be used as a guide in any situation where one process passes information to another. In particular, processes which drive input peripherals act as producers for those processes which consume the input, and processes which drive output peripherals act as consumers for those processes which produce the output.


## (3) Deadlock

As pointed out earlier, deadlock can occur whenever a set of processes compete for resources. As such it is a problem that we will leave for full discussion until chapter 8.

In this section we remark that deadlock may also occur because processes are waiting for each other to complete certain actions. As an example, consider two processes $A$ and $B$ which operate on semaphores $X$ and $Y$ as below.

| *process A* | *process B* |
|---|---|
| . | . |
| . | . |
| . | . |
| *wait(X);* | *wait(Y);* |
| . | . |
| . | . |
| . | . |
| *wait (Y);* | *wait(X);* |
| . | . |
| . | . |
| . | . |

If the initial values of $X$ and $Y$ are 1 then each process can complete its first *wait* operation, reducing the semaphore values to 0. Clearly, neither process can then proceed beyond its next *wait* operation, and deadlock prevails.

The situation is in fact analogous to that in which deadlock arises from competing resource requests. If a semaphore is regarded as a resource, and *wait* and *signal* operations regarded as claiming and releasing it, then deadlock has ensued because both $A$ and $B$ hold the resource required by the other. The 'shareability' of a semaphore is determined by its initial value: if the value is $n$ $(>1)$ the semaphore can be shared by $n$ processes; if it is 1 (as above) then the semaphore is unshareable.

A similar but more complex case of deadlock can be derived from the producer–consumer problem by reversing the order of the *wait* operations performed by the consumers. If the buffer is empty it is possible for a consumer to gain access to the buffer by executing 'wait (*buffer manipulation*)' and then to be suspended on 'wait (*item available*)'. The only way in which the consumer can be freed is for a producer to deposit an item in the buffer and execute 'signal (*item available*)'. However, no producer can gain access to the buffer since it is held by the blocked consumer. Hence deadlock results. Again the situation is analogous to that resulting from competing resource requests. In this case the resources are the buffer, held by the consumer, and a new item, held by a producer.

The lesson to be learned from these examples is that deadlock can occur as a result of an incorrectly ordered sequence of *wait* operations even when no explicit resource requests are being made. It may be salutary to realise that the deadlock threat inherent in the wrong solution to the producer–consumer problem would not be detected by the validation carried out in the last section.

Both the deadlock-free and deadlock-prone solutions satisfy relation 3.3, and thus appear equally correct by that criterion. Criteria for recognising deadlock in respect of resource allocation will be discussed in chapter 8; the recognition of deadlock (or lack of it) in a sequence of *wait* operations can be performed by an analysis similar to the following.

Consider the solution to the producer–consumer problem given in section (2) above. We shall show that it is in fact deadlock-free. Firstly we observe that the inner sections of the programs for the producers and consumers are simply critical sections protected by the semaphore *buffer manipulation*, and therefore in themselves possess no deadlock potential. Hence deadlock can prevail only if

(a)   no producer can pass *wait* (*space available*) and no consumer is in a position to execute *signal* (*space available*) (that is, no consumer is extracting);

and

(b)   no consumer can pass *wait* (*item available*) and no producer is in a position to execute *signal* (*item available*) (that is, no producer is depositing).

Condition (a), with relation 3.2, implies

$$nw \ (space \ available) = ns \ (space \ available) + N$$

and

$$nw \ (item \ available) = ns \ (space \ available)$$

Condition (b), with relation 3.2, implies

$$nw \ (item \ available) = ns \ (item \ available)$$

and

$$nw \ (space \ available) = ns \ (item \ available)$$

Putting these relations together we get

$$nw \ (space \ available) = nw \ (space \ available) + N$$

which is a contradiction (since $N > 0$).

A similar analysis for the case in which the order of *wait* operations in the consumer program is reversed is not possible, since the inner section of the program for the consumers is no longer a simple critical section (it now contains a *wait* operation). A more complex analysis (for example, Habermann, 1972; Lister, 1974) is needed to show that deadlock can in fact occur.

## 3.4 SUMMARY

In this chapter we have introduced the notion of a process, as opposed to a program, and have shown that it is a useful concept in the study of operating system characteristics. In particular we have seen that both concurrency and nondeterminacy can be described in terms of switching processors between processes. We have also introduced semaphores and the operations on them as a mechanism for inter–process communication, and have demonstrated that they are a sufficient tool for solving problems of mutual exclusion and synchronisation. Finally we have seen that it is possible in some cases to use certain relations about the values of semaphores to demonstrate that processes exhibit the properties we expect.

In the next chapter we shall use these tools to start the construction of our paper operating system.

# 4 *The System Nucleus*

In the last chapter we developed the concepts and tools needed to build the paper operating system outlined in chapter 1. As mentioned there, the paper operating system will resemble an onion in which each layer provides a set of functions dependent only on the layers within it. At the centre of the onion are the facilities provided by the hardware of the machine itself. The onion layers can be regarded as implementing successive virtual machines, so that the onion as a whole implements the virtual machine required by the user.

The major interface between the basic machine hardware and the operating system is provided by the system *nucleus*, which is the innermost layer of the onion. The purpose of the nucleus is to provide an environment in which processes can exist; this implies handling interrupts, switching processors between processes, and implementing mechanisms for inter-process communication. Before describing these functions in detail we shall look at the essential hardware required to support the operating system we are trying to build.

## 4.1 ESSENTIAL HARDWARE FACILITIES

### (1) Interrupt Mechanism

It was mentioned in chapter 2 that in order for I/O activities to be overlapped with central processing it must be possible to interrupt the running process when a peripheral transfer is complete. We therefore demand that our computer should provide an interrupt mechanism which at least saves the value of the program counter for the interrupted process and transfers control to a fixed location in memory. This location will be used as the start of a piece of program known as an *interrupt routine*, or *interrupt handler,* whose purpose is to determine the source of the interrupt and respond to it in an appropriate manner. We will describe the interrupt handler in section 4.4, and will discuss the various forms it can take according to the precise nature of the interrupt mechanism available.

(For the sake of completeness we mention that some computers, for example, the CDC CYBER, operate without an explicit interrupt mechanism. In such a computer one or more processors must be dedicated to monitoring the status of the I/O devices to detect when transfers are complete. In the case of the CYBER this function is performed by a number of so-called 'peripheral processors', while the CPU is relieved of all I/O handling. A restricted form of interrupt still exists, however, since the peripheral processors can force the CPU to jump to a different location.)

### (2) Memory Protection

When several processes are running concurrently it is necessary to protect the memory used by one process from unauthorised access by another. The protection mechanisms which must be built into the memory addressing hardware are described in detail in the next chapter; for the present we take their existence for granted.

### (3) Privileged Instruction Set

In order that concurrent processes cannot interfere with each other, part of the instruction set of the computer must be reserved for use by the operating system only. These privileged instructions perform such functions as

(a)  enabling and disabling interrupts
(b)  switching a processor between processes
(c)  accessing registers used by the memory protection hardware
(d)  performing input or output
(e)  halting a central processor

　　To distinguish between times when privileged instructions are or are not allowed, most computers operate in one of two modes, usually known as *supervisor mode* and *user mode*. Privileged instructions can be used only in supervisor mode. The switch from user to supervisor mode is made automatically in any of the following circumstances.

(a)  A user process calls on the operating system to execute some function requiring the use of a privileged instruction. Such a call is termed an *extracode*, or *supervisor call*.
(b)  An interrupt occurs.
(c)  An error condition occurs in a user process. The condition can be treated as an 'internal interrupt', and handled in the first instance by an interrupt routine.
(d)  An attempt is made to execute a privileged instruction while in user mode. The attempt can be regarded as a particular kind of error, and handled as in (c) above.

The switch from supervisor mode back to user mode is effected by an instruction which is itself privileged.

It should perhaps be mentioned that the scheme above, which involves two levels of privilege, is extended on some computers (for example, the ICL 2900 and Honeywell 645) to incorporate several levels. We shall defer discussion of such multilevel machines until chapter 9.

### (4) Real-time Clock

A hardware clock which interrupts at fixed intervals of real-time (that is, time as measured in the outside world rather than time received for computation by any particular process) is essential for the implementation of scheduling policies and for the accounting of resources consumed by the various users.

We shall assume from this point on that the machine on which we are building our paper operating system has the hardware facilities outlined above. More precisely, since we allow the possibility of including several central processors in a single configuration, we shall assume that each processor has facilities (1) to (3) and that there is a single real-time clock which can interrupt each processor. In addition we shall restrict ourselves to *tightly coupled* configurations in which the processors are identical and share a common memory. This excludes consideration of computer networks, in which the processors have separate memories and communicate by some form of data transmission, and of systems in which dissimilar processors are organised so as to share a workload in a way best suited to their particular characteristics. The former topic merits a book on its own; the latter is still a fertile field for research in which no clear trends have yet emerged.

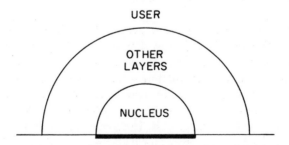

*Figure 4.1 Structure of the paper operating system*

### 4.2 OUTLINE OF THE NUCLEUS

The relationship between the nucleus and the rest of the operating system is illustrated in figure 4.1. The horizontal line at the base of the diagram represents the computer hardware; the thickened portion of this line is the privileged instruction set, whose use we restrict to the nucleus. (Exceptions to this rule are some privileged instructions concerned with memory protection and I/O, discussed in later chapters.)

The nucleus consists of three pieces of program

(1)     the *first-level interrupt handler*, which performs the initial handling of all interrupts;
(2)     the *dispatcher*, which switches the central processors between processes;
(3)     two procedures (routines) which implement the inter-process communication primitives *wait* and *signal* described in chapter 3. These procedures are called via extracodes in the processes concerned.

Because the nucleus is built directly on the basic hardware we can expect it to be the most heavily machine-dependent part of an operating system. Indeed it is probably the only part of the operating system which need be written substantially in assembly language: with a few small exceptions, mainly related to I/O, the other layers can be most conveniently coded in a high-level language. Suitable systems programming languages, to which the reader may care to refer, are BCPL (Richards, 1969) and BLISS (Wulf *et al.*, 1971). Other languages, like Concurrent Pascal (Hansen, 1975) and Modula (Wirth, 1977), are intended specifically for writing operating systems, though they impose certain constraints on the system designer. The restriction of assembly language to one small (probably no more than 400 instructions) part of the operating system, made possible by the system's hierarchical structure, can contribute greatly towards realising the goal of an error-free, comprehensible, and maintainable product.

### 4.3 REPRESENTATION OF PROCESSES

The programs within the nucleus are responsible for maintaining the environment in which processes exist. Consequently they are required to operate on some data structure which is the physical representation of all processes within the system. The nature of this data structure is the concern of the current section.

Each process can be represented by a *process descriptor* (sometimes known as a *control block* or *state vector*) which is an area of memory containing all relevant information about the process. The composition of this information will become apparent as we progress; for the present we include in it some identification of the process (the *process name*) and an indication of the process's *status*. A process can have one of three principal statuses: it may be *running*, which means that it is executing on a processor; it may be *runnable*, meaning that it could run if a processor were allocated to it; or it may be *unrunnable*, meaning that it could not use a processor even if one were allocated. The most common reason for a process being unrunnable is that it is waiting for the completion of a peripheral transfer. The status of a process is an essential piece of information for the dispatcher when it comes to allocate a central processor.

We shall refer to a process which is running on a central processor as the *current process* for that processor; the number of current processes within the system at any time is of course less than or equal to the number of processors available.

A further part of the process descriptor can be used to store all information about the process which needs to be saved when it loses control of a processor. This information, required for subsequent resumption of the process, includes the values of all machine registers, such as program counter, accumulators, and index registers, which could be changed by another process. It also includes the values of any registers used in addressing the memory owned by the process (see chapter 5). We call the whole of this information the *volatile environment* of the process (other names in the literature are *context block* and *process state*). More formally, the volatile environment of a process can be defined as that subset of the modifiable shared facilities of the system which are accessible to the process.

The process descriptor of each process is linked into a *process structure*, which acts as a description of all processes within the system. For the present we shall adopt an elementary form of process structure, in which the process descriptors are linked into a simple list. The process structure is the first data structure we have introduced into our operating system; since it will be by no means the last, we also introduce a *central table* whose purpose is to serve as a means of access to all system structures. The central table will contain a pointer to each data structure, and may also be used to hold any other global information, such as the date, time of day, and system version number, which might from time to time be required. The central table and process structure are illustrated in figure 4.2.

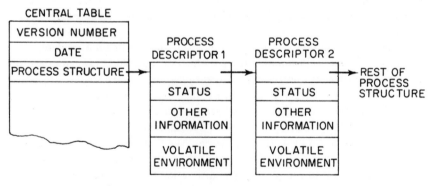

*Figure 4.2 Central table and process structure*

## 4.4 THE FIRST-LEVEL INTERRUPT HANDLER

The first-level interrupt handler (FLIH) is the part of the operating system which is responsible for responding to signals both from the outside world (interrupts) and from within the computing system itself (error traps and extracodes). We shall refer collectively to both types of signal as interrupts and use the adjectives 'external' and 'internal' to distinguish between them where necessary. The function of the FLIH is twofold

(1)    to determine the source of the interrupt
(2)    to service the interrupt

We have already stated in section 4.1 that the computer's interrupt mechanism is responsible for saving at least the value of the program counter for the inter-rupted process. It must also be ensured that other registers required by the FLIH which may be being used by the interrupted process are appropriately saved. If this is not done by the interrupt mechanism it must be performed as the first operation of the FLIH itself. Because the FLIH is a relatively simple program operating in a dedicated area of memory the set of registers involved will not be large, perhaps only a single accumulator. It will certainly be considerably smaller than the volatile environment of the interrupted process, which need not be saved in its entirety since the process may be resumed once the interrupt has been serviced.

An alternative strategy to saving register values, adopted for example on the ICL System 4, the RCA Spectra 70, and some of the PDP-11 range, is to provide an extra set of registers for use in supervisor mode only. The FLIH can use these registers and leave those of the interrupted process intact.

Determination of the source of the interrupt can be performed more or less easily depending on the hardware provided. In the case of the most primitive hardware, in which all interrupts transfer control to the same location, identi-fication must be achieved by a sequence of tests on the status flags of all possible sources. This sequence, often called a *skip chain*, is illustrated in figure 4.3. It is clearly advantageous to code the skip chain so that the most frequent sources of interrupts occur near its head.

On some computers (for example the PDP-11) the skip chain is rendered unnecessary by the inclusion of hardware which distinguishes between interrupt sources by transferring control to a different location for each source. This reduces the time to identify an interrupt at the cost of the extra interrupt locations required. A compromise arrangement employed on several computers, including the IBM 370 series, is to provide a small number of interrupt locations each of which is shared by a group of devices. The first stage of interrupt identi-fication is then achieved by hardware, and a short skip chain starting at each location is sufficient to complete it. The distinction between external interrupts, error traps, and extracodes is often made in this way. The interrupt mechanism, as on the IBM 370, may give further aids to identification by planting information about the interrupt in some fixed memory location.

Interrupts to a central processor are normally inhibited when it switches from user to supervisor mode. This ensures that the values of registers saved on entry to the FLIH cannot be overwritten by a subsequent interrupt occurring before the FLIH is left. An interrupt which occurs while the interrupt mechanism is disabled is held pending until the mechanism is re-enabled on resumption of user mode. This arrangement becomes inoperable in situations where some peripheral devices require response far more quickly than others if, for example, data is not to be lost. In these cases it is convenient to introduce the notion of *priority* among the various interrupt sources, and to allow an interrupt routine to be itself interrupted by a request for service from a device of a higher priority. Some computers (for example the IBM 370) allow this to be done by selectively disabling interrupts within the FLIH; when the FLIH is servicing an interrupt it disables all those of equal or lower priority. Care must of course be taken to store the program registers of the interrupted process in different locations according to the priority level of the interrupt received. Alternatively, the interrupt hardware may itself distinguish between various priority levels, trans- ferring control to and saving registers at different locations for each level. An interrupt at one level automatically inhibits others at the same or lower levels. The DEC System-10 is an example of a machine with this kind of priority interrupt mechanism, having seven priority levels in all.

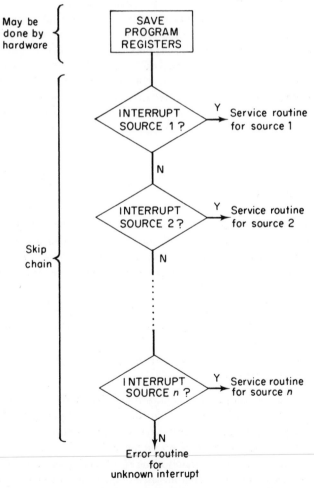

*Figure 4.3 Interrupt identification by a skip chain*

The second function of the FLIH, that of servicing an interrupt, is clearly dependent on the type of interrupt involved. We shall give details in chapter 6 of service routines for I/O devices, and in chapter 11 of handling error traps. At this stage we remark only that because the interrupt routines run in supervisor mode with interrupts wholly or partially inhibited it is desirable to keep them as short as possible. In general each routine will perform some minimal action, for example transferring a character from an input device into a buffer, and hand over responsibility for further action, such as reacting to the character received, to a process which runs in normal user mode.

It is important to note that the occurrence of an interrupt, either external or internal, will often alter the status of some process. For instance, a process which has requested a peripheral transfer and which is unrunnable while the transfer is in progress will be made runnable again by the interrupt which occurs at its completion. Again, certain extracodes, such as a *wait* operation on a zero-valued semaphore or a request for I/O, will result in the current process being unable to continue. In all cases the change of status is effected by the interrupt routine changing the status entry in the process descriptor of the process concerned.

A consequence of the status change is that the process which was running on the processor concerned before the interrupt occurred may not be the most suitable to run afterwards. It may be the case, for example, that the interrupt makes runnable a process which in some sense has a higher priority than the currently running one. The question of when to switch a central processor between processes, and which process to favour, is considered in the next section.

## 4.5 THE DISPATCHER

It is the function of the dispatcher (sometimes known as the *low-level scheduler*) to allocate the central processors among the various processes in the system. It is entered whenever a current process cannot continue, or whenever there are grounds to suppose that a processor might be better employed elsewhere. These occasions may be detailed as follows

(1)    after an external interrupt which changes the status of some process;
(2)    after an extracode which results in the current process being temporarily unable to continue;
(3)    after an error trap which causes suspension of the current process while the error is dealt with.

These occasions are all special cases of interrupts; that is, they are all interrupts which alter the status of some process. For the sake of simplicity we do not distinguish them from those interrupts, such as a *wait* operation on a positive-valued semaphore, which have no effect on the status of any process; we say, in effect, that the dispatcher is ultimately entered after *all* interrupts. The overhead in entering the dispatcher on occasions when no process status has changed is more than offset by the advantages gained from a uniform treatment of all interrupts.

The operation of the dispatcher is quite simple.


(1)   Is the current process on this processor still the most suitable to run? If so then return control to it at the point indicated by the program counter stored by the interrupt hardware. If not, then ...

(2)   Save the volatile environment of the current process in its process descriptor.

(3)   Retrieve the volatile environment of the most suitable process from its process descriptor.

(4)   Transfer control to it at the location indicated by the restored program counter.


To determine the most suitable process to run it is sufficient to order all runnable processes by some priority. The assignment of priorities to processes is not a function of the dispatcher but of the high-level scheduler to be described in chapter 8. For the present we remark that priorities are calculated according to such factors as the amount of resources required, the length of time since the process last ran, and the relative importance of the originating user. As far as the dispatcher is concerned the process priorities are given *a priori*.

In our paper operating system we link the process descriptors of all runnable processes into a queue ordered by decreasing priority, so that the most eligible process is at its head. We call this queue the *processor queue*, illustrated in figure 4.4. Thus the role of the dispatcher is to run the first process on the processor queue which is not already running on some other processor. This may. or may not be the same process as was running before the dispatcher was invoked.

We note in passing that the introduction of the processor queue means that the action taken by an interrupt routine to make a process runnable is now two-fold. Firstly it must alter the status entry in the process descriptor and secondly it must link the process descriptor into the processor queue at the position indicated by its priority. We shall see in the next section that this operation can conveniently be done by executing a *signal* operation on a semaphore on which the process concerned has executed *wait*.

It is of course possible that at a particular moment the processor queue contains fewer processes than there are processors, perhaps because several processes are waiting for input or output. This situation, which is probably the result of a poor high-level scheduling decision, implies that there is no work for some central processors to do. Rather than allowing a processor to loop within the dispatcher it is convenient to introduce an extra process, called the *null process*, which has the lowest priority and is always runnable. The null process may be nothing more than an idle loop, or it may perform some useful function such as executing processor test programs. It has been known for the null process

to be used for such esoteric purposes as solving chess endgame problems or
calculating the decimal expansion of $\pi$. Its position at the end of the processor
queue is shown in figure 4.4.

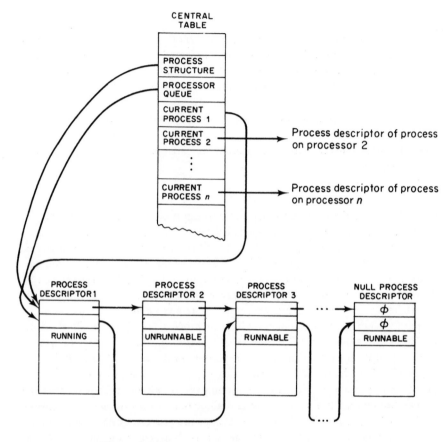

*Figure 4.4 Process structure and processor queue*

The operation of the dispatcher can now be summarised as follows.

(1)   Is the current process on this processor still the first non-running process
      on the processor queue? If so then resume it. If not then ...
(2)   Save the volatile environment of the current process.
(3)   Restore the volatile environment of the first non-running process in the
      processor queue.
(4)   Resume running this process.

Before leaving the dispatcher we should point out that we have chosen a very
simple structure for the runnable processes. Many operating systems divide the
runnable processes into several classes, distinguished by such criteria as resources

required, the maximum waiting time to be tolerated, or the amount of processor time to be allowed before pre-emption. The DEC System-10 monitor for example has three processor queues, one each for processes which are allowed 2 seconds, 0.25 seconds, and 0.02 seconds respectively before pre-emption. Each queue is serviced on a first come, first served basis, with the shorter pre-emption time queues having the higher priority. A process is originally placed in the 0.02 second queue; if it runs for the whole of its allowed quantum it is relegated to the 0.25 second queue, and similarly, if it runs for the whole of its increased quantum it is relegated to the 2 second queue. The effect is to ensure that processes associated with on-line terminals, which typically have low processor requirements, receive a rapid service, whereas processor bound jobs receive longer but less frequent attention. We shall say more about this when we discuss scheduling in chapter 8.

We conclude this section by summarising the relationship between the FLIH and the dispatcher in the diagram below.

| Interrupt mechanism | Save program counter<br>Save other registers (optional)<br>Enter FLIH |
| FLIH | Save program registers (if not done above)<br>Identify interrupt (aided by hardware)<br>Enter some service routine |
| Service routine | Service interrupt, possibly altering status of some process |
| Dispatcher | Processor switch necessary? If not, resume interrupted process<br>Save volatile environment of current process<br>Restore volatile environment of first eligible process in processor queue<br>Transfer control to new process |

## 4.6 IMPLEMENTATION OF *wait* AND *signal*

The final part of the nucleus is the implementation of some form of inter-process communication mechanism. As indicated in chapter 3 we shall use the operations *wait* and *signal* as our communication primitives, a choice which is based on the widespread understanding and ease of implementation of semaphores. Other communication mechanisms, which are perhaps less easy to implement but less prone to misuse, can be found in the literature (Hoare, 1974; Campbell and Habermann, 1974; Hansen, 1978).

*Wait* and *signal* are included in the nucleus because

(1)　they must be available to all processes, and hence must be implemented at a low level;

(2)    the *wait* operation may result in a process being blocked, causing an entry to the dispatcher to reallocate the processor. Hence the *wait* operation must have access to the dispatcher;

(3)    a convenient way for an interrupt routine to awaken (make runnable) a process is to execute *signal* on a semaphore on which the process has executed *wait*. Hence *signal* must be accessible to the interrupt routines.

The operations we have to implement (see chapter 3) are

> *wait*(s)    :    **when** $s > 0$ **do** decrement $s$
>
> *signal*(s)   :    increment $s$

where $s$ is any semaphore. We develop our implementation as follows.

### (1) Blocking and Unblocking

The *wait* operation implies that processes are blocked when a semaphore has value 0 and freed when a *signal* operation increases the value to 1. The natural way to implement this is to associate with each semaphore a *semaphore queue*. When a process performs an 'unsuccessful' *wait* operation (that is, it operates on a zero-value semaphore) it is added to the semaphore queue and made unrunnable. Conversely, when a *signal* operation is performed on a semaphore some process can be taken off the semaphore queue (unless empty) and made runnable again. The semaphore must therefore be implemented with two components: an integer and a queue pointer (which may be null).

At this point our implementation is as follows

> *wait*(s)    :    **if** $s \neq 0$ **then** $s := s - 1$
>                     **else** add process to semaphore queue and make unrunnable;
>
> *signal*(s)   :    **if** queue empty **then** $s := s + 1$
>                     **else** remove some process from semaphore queue and make runnable;

Note that the semaphore need not be incremented within *signal* if a process is to be freed, since the freed process would immediately have to decrement the semaphore again in completing its *wait* operation.

### (2) Queueing and Dequeueing

We have said nothing yet about which process is lucky enough to be removed from the semaphore queue after a *signal* operation. Nor have we stated whether a process which is added to the queue on an unsuccessful *wait* operation should be added at the head, tail, or somewhere in the middle. In other words we have not yet specified the queue organisation.

For most semaphores a simple first in, first out queue is adequate, since it ensures that all blocked processes are eventually freed. In some cases it may be preferable to order the queue on some other basis, perhaps by a priority similar to that used in the processor queue. This latter organisation ensures that processes with high processor priority do not languish for long periods of time on a sema-phore queue. The important point is that different semaphores may require different queue organisations, so that an extra component must be included in the semaphore implementation to indicate which queue organisation applies. This component may simply be a coded description of the queue organisation, or in more complex cases it may be a pointer to a small piece of program which will perform the queueing and dequeueing operations. The structure of a semaphore in our implementation is shown in figure 4.5.

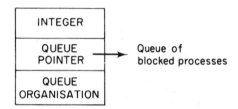

*Figure 4.5 Structure of a semaphore*

### (3) Processor Allocation

Both *wait* and *signal* may alter the status of a process, the former by making it unrunnable and the latter by doing the opposite. An exit must therefore be made to the dispatcher for a decision on which process to run next. In cases where no process status has changed (that is, a *wait* on a positive valued semaphore or a *signal* on a semaphore with an empty queue) the dispatcher will resume the current process since it will still be the first non-running process in the processor queue. It is arguable that in this case the return from *wait* or *signal* should be directly to the current process rather than via the dispatcher; the resulting gain in efficiency would be at the expense of a slight extra complexity in the code for *wait* and *signal*. In this discussion we shall opt for simplicity over efficiency, while recognising that the opposite viewpoint may be equally valid.

### (4) Indivisibility

As pointed out in chapter 3 both *wait* and *signal* must be indivisable operations in the sense that only one process can be allowed to execute them at any time. Hence they must both be implemented as procedures which begin with some kind of *lock* operation and end with an *unlock* operation. On a single processor configuration the lock operation can most easily be implemented by disabling the interrupt mechanism. This ensures that a process cannot lose control of the central processor while executing *wait* and *signal* since there is no way in which it can be interrupted. The unlock operation is performed by simply re-enabling the interrupts. On a machine with several central processors this procedure is inadequate since it is possible for two processes simultaneously to enter *wait* or *signal* by running on separate processors. In this case we need some other mechanism, such as a 'test and set' instruction. This is an instruction which tests and modifies the content of a memory location in a single operation. During execution of the instruction attempts by other processes to access the location are inhibited.

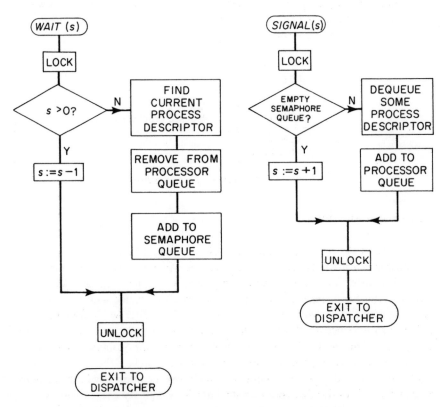

*Figure 4.6 Implementation of wait and signal*

The idea is that a particular location is used as a flag (similar to the variable *gate* in section 3.3) which indicates whether entry to the *wait* and *signal* procedures is allowed. If the flag is non-zero (say) entry is permitted, otherwise it is not. The lock operation consists of executing a test and set instruction on the flag, which determines its value and at the same time sets it to zero. If the value of the flag is non-zero then the process proceeds, otherwise it loops on the test and set instruction until the process currently inside the *wait* or *signal* procedure unlocks the flag by setting it to some non-zero value. Note that difficulties similar to those which arose in respect of the variable *gate* in section

3.3 are avoided by implementing the entire test and set instruction as a single indivisible operation. This lock/unlock mechanism is adopted on many computers, such as the IBM 370 series.

An alternative to test and set, adopted on the Burroughs 6000 series and the Plessey 250, is an instruction to interchange the contents of two memory locations. The lock operation starts by interchanging the values of a flag and a location which has previously been set to zero. The value of this second location is then examined to see whether entry is permitted, while any other process trying to gain entry will find the zero left by the interchange. A process which finds after the interchange that the flag was zero simply repeats the lock operation until the flag is made non-zero by some other process executing an unlock operation.

It should be noted that both these mechanisms imply some form of *busy waiting*. That is, a process which cannot pass the lock operation ties up its processor in a tight loop repeatedly trying the operation until the flag becomes unset. So long as the *wait* and *signal* procedures are simple the length of time involved in busy waiting should be quite short.

It is worth emphasising that the lock and unlock operations cannot be used as a substitute for *wait* and *signal*. The busy waiting or interrupt inhibition used to implement the lock operation would not be acceptable over the time scale for which processes can be delayed by a *wait* operation. The table below shows the conceptually different levels at which the two kinds of operation exist.

|  | *Wait* and *Signal* | Lock and Unlock |
| --- | --- | --- |
| Purpose | General process synchronisation | Mutual exclusion of processes from *wait* and *signal* procedures |
| Implementation level | Software | Hardware |
| Delaying mechanism | Queueing | Busy waiting/interrupt inhibition |
| Typical delay time | Several seconds | Several microseconds |

The result of the foregoing discussion is that we can implement *wait* and *signal* as two related procedures as shown in figure 4.6. The procedures will be called by extracodes which are part of the instruction repertoire of all processes.

We have now completed the system nucleus, which consists of the first-level interrupt handler, the dispatcher and the procedures for *wait* and *signal*, all running in supervisor mode.

# 5 *Memory Management*

Memory management is the next layer of our 'onion'. We put it next to the nucleus because unless a process possesses some memory there is very little it can do. It certainly cannot execute, since there is no room for the associated program, nor can it perform input or output without space for buffers.

In this chapter we shall first of all discuss the objectives of memory management and introduce the concept of virtual memory. We shall describe ways in which virtual memory can be implemented, and then discuss various policies for regulating the implementation. Finally, we shall see how memory management can be included in our paper operating system.

## 5.1 OBJECTIVES

The objectives of memory management are fourfold.

### (1) Relocation

In a multiprogrammed computer the available memory will generally be shared at any given time between a number of processes, and it is not possible for the individual programmer to know in advance what other programs will be resident in memory when his own program is run. This means that he does not know at the time he writes the program precisely whereabouts in memory it will be located, and hence he cannot write the program in terms of absolute memory addresses. If the memory allocated to his program remained fixed during its entire run, then it would of course be possible to transform symbolic or relative addresses into absolute addresses at the time the program was loaded, but in fact this is seldom the case. As processes run to completion the space they use becomes free for other processes, and it may be necessary to move processes around in memory in order to make the best use of the space available. In particular, it may be desirable to move processes so that small non-contiguous areas of free memory become compacted into a larger, more useful, single area. Thus the region of memory allocated to a process may change during the process's lifetime, and the system must be responsible for transforming the addresses used by the programmer into the actual addresses in which the process is physically located.

## (2) Protection

When several processes are sharing memory it is of course essential for their integrity that none of them is permitted to alter the contents of memory locations which are currently allocated to the others. Compile time checks on program addresses are an inadequate protection since most languages allow the dynamic calculation of addresses at run time, for example by computing array subscripts or pointers into data structures. Hence all memory references generated by a process must be checked at run time to ensure that they refer only to the memory space allocated to that process. (Strictly speaking, only write accesses need be checked, but if privacy of information is required then read accesses must also be checked.)

## (3) Logical Organisation

The traditional computer has a one-dimensional, or linear address space in that addresses are numbered sequentially from zero to the upper limit of memory. While this organisation closely mirrors the hardware of the machine it does not really reflect the ways in which programs are usually written. Most programs are structured in some way — into modules or procedures — and refer to distinct areas of modifiable or unmodifiable data. For example, a compiler may be written with separate modules for lexical analysis, syntax analysis, and code generation, and among its data areas may be a table of reserved words (unmodifiable) and a symbol table (modified as new identifiers are encountered during compilation). If the logical divisions into program and data are reflected in a corresponding *segmentation* of address space then several advantages accrue. Firstly, it is possible for segments to be coded independently and for all references from one segment to another to be filled in by the system at run time; secondly, it is possible with little extra overhead to give different degrees of protection (for example, read only, execute only) to different segments; and thirdly, it is possible to introduce mechanisms by which segments can be shared among processes.

## (4) Physical Organisation

Historically, the general desire for large amounts of storage space and the high cost of fast memory have led to the almost universal adoption of two-level storage systems. The compromise between speed and cost is typically achieved by supplementing a small amount (up to 256K words) of direct access main memory by a much larger amount (several million words) of secondary memory, or backing store. Until recently main memory was constructed from magnetic cores, while backing store consisted of drums or discs; advances in technology have resulted in many semiconductor main memories (for example CDC CYBER large IBM 370) and some backing stores which consist partially of slow core.

Since in typical systems only information in main memory can be accessed directly, the organisation of the flow of information between main and secondary memories is obviously of prime importance. It is of course possible to rest the onus of organisation on the individual programmer, making him responsible for moving sections of program or data to or from main memory as required. Indeed, in the early days of computing this is what was done, and the technique of *overlay programming* — writing sections of program which overlaid themselves in memory — became an art in itself. However, there are two sound reasons which militate against such an approach. The first is that the programmer does not want to expend a great deal of effort in writing complicated overlays: he is too interested in solving his own problems to waste energy on side issues. Clever compilers can help by automatically generating overlay code at appropriate points in the program, but in many cases the compiler does not have sufficient information to know when the overlays will be required. The second reason is that because of dynamic relocation the programmer does not know at the time of writing how much space will be available or whereabouts in memory that space will be. Overlay programming thus becomes impracticable.

It is clear from these arguments that the task of moving information between the two levels of memory should be a system responsibility. How this responsibility can be carried out is discussed later in this chapter.

### 5.2 VIRTUAL MEMORY

The objectives listed above can be achieved by the conceptually simple (and pleasingly elegant) device of using an address translation mechanism, or *address map*, to transform the addresses used by the programmer into the corresponding physical memory locations actually allocated to the program. The maintenance of the address map is a system function, and possible implementations are discussed in the next section. The crucial point at this stage is the distinction between *program addresses* — addresses used by the programmer — and the physical *memory locations* into which they are mapped. The range of program addresses is known as the *address space* (or *name space*); the range of memory locations in the computer is the *memory space*. If the address space is denoted by $N$, and the memory space by $M$, then the address map can be denoted by

$$f \ : \ N \to M$$

On current computers the memory space is linear — that is, the memory locations are numbered sequentially from zero — and its size is equal to the amount of main memory included in the configuration. We shall see that the address space, however, need not be linear, and depending on the particular implementation of the address map its size may be smaller than, equal to, or greater than that of the memory space.

An alternative way of looking at the address map is to regard it as a means of allowing the programmer to use a range of program addresses which may be quite different from the range of memory locations available. Thus the programmer 'sees', and programs for, a *virtual memory* whose characteristics differ from those of the real memory. The address map is designed so as to produce a virtual memory convenient for the programmer, and so as to achieve some or all of the objectives listed in the previous section. The provision of virtual memory is a good example of the transformation (discussed in chapter 1) of the basic computer into a more convenient virtual machine.

In the next section we shall describe various virtual memories and the address maps which provide them.

## 5.3 IMPLEMENTATION OF VIRTUAL MEMORY

### (1) Base and Limit Registers

The first two objectives listed in section 5.1, namely relocation and protection, can be achieved by a fairly simple address map as follows.

When a process is loaded into memory the address of the lowest location used is placed in a *base register* (or *datum register*), and all program addresses are interpreted as being relative to this *base address*. The address map thus consists simply of adding the program address to the base address to produce the corresponding memory location; that is

$$f(a) = B + a$$

where $a$ is the program address, and $B$ is the base address of the process.

Relocation is accomplished by simply moving the process and resetting the base address to the appropriate value. Protection of memory space among processes can be achieved by including a second register — the *limit register* — which contains the address of the highest location which a particular process is permitted to access. The address map (see figure 5.1) performed by the memory addressing hardware then proceeds according to the following scheme

(a)   if $a < 0$ then memory violation
(b)   $a' := B + a$
(c)   if $a' > limit$ then memory violation
(d)   $a'$ is required location

It is worth noting that the address space mapped by this scheme is linear, and its size, being the difference between the base and limit registers, is necessarily less than or equal to the size of the memory space. Thus objectives (3) and (4) of section 5.1 are not achieved.

In order that the address mapping operation shall not be prohibitively time consuming the base and limit registers must be implemented in fast hardware. The cost of the registers can be reduced, and the mapping speeded up, by removing the lower order bits, implying that the size of the address space must be a multiple of $2^n$ (where $n$ is the number of bits removed). On the smaller

*Figure 5.1 Address map for base and limit registers*

ICL 1900 machines the number of bits removed is 6; on the DEC System-10 (KA-10) it is 10.

A slight variation on the base–limit scheme is to use the limit register to hold the *length* of the memory space rather than its upper limit. In this case the address map is

(a)    if $a < 0$ or $a > length$ then memory violation
(b)    $a' := B + a$
(c)    $a'$ is required location

The advantage is that the limit check does not depend on the result of the additition, so both the checks and the addition can be performed in parallel. (The addition is aborted if a memory violation occurs.)

It is impracticable, for economic reasons, to provide a pair of base and limit registers for each process which may be present in memory. Instead, a single pair of registers is provided for each processor, and is loaded with the base and limit addresses of the currently active process. These values form part of the volatile environment of the process and are stored when the process is suspended.

To allow for the use of re-entrant or 'pure' procedures it is necessary to elaborate on the base-limit mechanism by providing two pairs of registers rather than one. One pair is used to demarcate the memory space occupied by the re-entrant code, and the values in them are common to all processes using the code; the other pair is used to demarcate the data areas associated with the code, and hold different values for each process concerned. The older DEC System-10 is an example of a machine employing this technique.

## (2) Paging

In the base–limit scheme described above, the size of the address space is necessarily less than or equal to that of the memory space. If we wish to give the programmer a virtual memory which is larger than the available physical memory, thus relieving him of the burden of writing overlays, then we must devise an address map which apparently abolishes the distinction between main and secondary memory. The concept of the *one-level store*, in which secondary memory is made to appear as an extension of main memory, was first introduced on the Atlas computer at Manchester University around 1960, and has since had a profound influence on computer design.

The one-level store can be realised by the technique of *paging*, whereby the virtual address space is divided into *pages* of equal size (on Atlas 512 words), and the main memory is similarly divided into *page frames* of the same size. The page frames are shared between the processes currently in the system, so that at any time a given process will have a few pages resident in main memory (its *active* pages) and the rest resident in secondary memory (its *inactive* pages). The paging mechanism has two functions

(a) to perform the address mapping operation; that is, to determine which page a program address refers to, and find which page frame, if any, the page currently occupies;

(b) to transfer pages from secondary memory to main memory when required, and to transfer them back to secondary memory when they are no longer being used.

We describe these functions in turn.

In order to determine which page a program address refers to, the high order bits of the address are interpreted as a page number and the low order bits as the word number within the page. Thus if the page size is $2^n$ then the bottom $n$ bits of the address represent the word number, and the remaining bits the page number. The total number of bits in the address is sufficient to address the entire virtual memory. For example, on Atlas the program address was 20 bits long, giving a virtual memory of $2^{20}$ words; the page size was 512 words ($2^9$), and so the bottom 9 bits represented the word number and the top 11 bits represented the page number. The total number of pages in the virtual memory was therefore $2^{11}$ (as opposed to 32 page frames in the original physical memory).

It is worth emphasising that the division of the address into word and page number is a function of the hardware and is transparent to the programmer; as far as he is concerned he is programming in a large sequential address space.

The address map from page and word number to physical memory location is made by means of a *page table*, the $p$th entry of which contains the location $p'$ of the page frame containing page number $p$. (The possibility that the $p$th page is not in main memory will be dealt with in a moment.) The word number, $w$, is added to $p'$ to obtain the required location (see figure 5.2). The address map is therefore

$$f(a) = f(p,w) = p' + w$$

where program address $a$, page number $p$, and word number $w$ are related to the page size $Z$ by

$$p \ = \ \text{integral part of } (a/Z)$$
$$w \ = \ \text{remainder of } (a/Z)$$

Since the number of pages frames (amount of real memory) allocated to a process will usually be less than the number of pages it actually uses, it is quite possible that a program address will refer to a page which is not currently held in main memory. In this case the corresponding entry in the page table will be empty, and a 'page fault' interrupt is given if an attempt is made to access it. The interrupt causes the paging mechanism to initiate the transfer of the missing page from secondary to main memory and update the page table accordingly. The current process is made unrunnable until the transfer is complete. The location of the page in secondary memory can be held in a separate table or in the page table itself. In the latter case a 'presence bit' in each page table entry is needed to indicate whether or not the page is present in main memory and whether the address field is to be interpreted as a page frame address or a backing store location.

*Figure 5.2 Simple address map for paging*

If no empty page frame exists at the time the page fault occurs then some other page must be moved into secondary memory in order to make room for the incoming page. The choice of which page to swap out in this way is the result of a *page turning algorithm*; we discuss various algorithms in later sections. For the present we remark that information required by the page turning algorithm can be held in a few bits added to each page table entry (the shaded section of figure 5.2). This information might be

(a)    how many times the page has been referenced
(b)    the time the page was last referenced
(c)    whether the page has been written to

It should perhaps be made clear that the entire address mapping operation is performed by hardware except when a page has to be brought in from secondary memory. In this case the application of the page turning algorithm and the updating of the page table are performed by software.

The foregoing discussion gives a general outline of how paging works; in practice several modifications must be made to obtain a viable implementation. In particular, in the system as described the time required for each memory reference is effectively doubled by the necessity of first accessing the page table. A way of overcoming this would be to keep the page table in a set of fast registers rather than in ordinary memory. However, the size of the page table is proportional to the size of the address space and hence the number of registers required would be too large to be economically feasible. The solution to the problem is to adopt a quite different technique for accessing active pages. This technique involves the addition to the machine of an *associative store*, which consists of a small set of *page address registers* (PARs), each of which contains the page number of an active page. The PARs have the property that they can be searched *simultaneously* for the page number occurring in a particular program address. For example, in figure 5.3 the program address 3243 is split up into page number 3 and word number 243. (For convenience the page size is assumed to be 1000.) The page number is then simultaneously compared with the contents of all the PARs, and is found to correspond to that of PAR 5. This indicates that page number 3 currently occupies page frame 5 and so the required memory location is 5243.

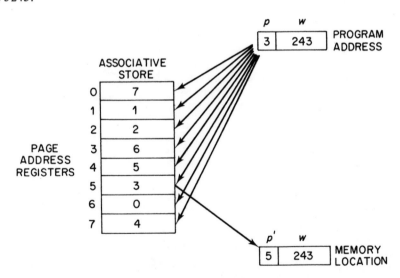

*Figure 5.3 Mapping by means of associative store*

The use of an associative store reduces the overhead of the address map to about 50 nanoseconds, compared with about 500 nanoseconds for a page table held in main memory.

In order that all active pages should be referenced by a PAR one needs as many PARs as there are page frames in memory. This is possible in systems with small memories (for example, Atlas), but on larger systems, it is not economically feasible to provide all the PARs required. (One might, however, expect that economic arguments will change as technology develops.) In such cases a compromise can be reached by holding a complete page table in memory for each process, and by using a small associative store to reference a few pages of the most recently active processes. In this case the page frame referred to by each PAR is no longer implicit in the PAR's position within the associative store, but must be included as an extra field in the PAR itself. The memory addressing hardware then performs the address mapping operation shown in figure 5.4. As before, software intervention is required only for page replacement.

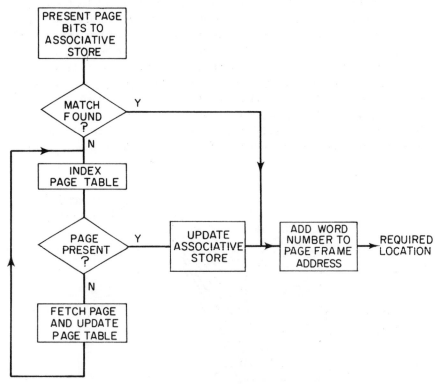

*Figure 5.4 Address mapping operation for paging with
a small associative store*

One problem not illustrated by figure 5.4 is that of distinguishing in the associative store between pages belonging to the current process and pages belonging to other processes. One solution, adopted on the MU5 computer, is to extend the PARs to include process identification as well as page number. Each address presented to the associative store must then include the process identification as well as the page bits. An alternative solution is to extend the PARs by a single bit which is set to one in entries belonging to the current process and to zero elsewhere. This solution necessarily implies having a separate associative store for each processor in the configuration. (This is probably advisable in any case in order that the memory addressing logic does not form a bottleneck between processors and memory.)

It is clearly desirable that the associative store contains the page numbers of those pages which are most likely to be referenced. Unfortunately there is no general algorithm for ensuring that this is so (compare section 5.4 on the traffic of pages between main and secondary memories); in practice the associative store is usually filled cyclically with the addresses of the most recently referenced pages. This rather crude algorithm is in fact quite effective; depending on memory size a store of only 8 or 16 registers can be expected to give an average hit rate of better than 99 per cent.

As a final observation on the mechanics of paging it is worth pointing out the large amount of main memory which can be occupied by the page tables themselves. For example, on the paged version of the DEC System-10 the address space consists of 512 pages of 512 words each; this implies a page table of 256 words (entries are packed two to a word) for each process in memory. In fact the page table is placed in a page of its own, the other half of which is used to hold the process descriptor.

The size of page tables can be reduced to the number of pages actually used, rather than the number in the address space, by accessing them by hashing rather than by indexing. The idea is that instead of containing an entry for every page in the address space the page table refers only to those pages which have been used. Each time a new page is brought into main memory the page number and corresponding page frame address are entered in the table at a point determined by a suitable hash function. The same hash function can then be used to locate the page during the address mapping operation. The penalty paid for the reduction in size of the page table is an increase in memory access time for some references. The increase is due to two factors: first there is the time required to compute the hash function itself, and second, in the case that the hashed entries in the page table collide, it may be necessary to access the table more than once before the required page is located. Despite this the scheme can be made viable by using an associative store, which can reduce the number of occasions on which the page table is referenced to about one per cent of the total, and by performing the hashing operation by hardware.

## (3) Segmentation

The third objective of section 5.1, namely the organisation of address space to reflect logical divisions in program and data, can be achieved by using the technique of *segmentation*. The idea is that the address space is divided into *segments*, each segment corresponding to a procedure, program module, or collection of data. This can be done in a simple way by adding several pairs of base and limit registers to each processor so that the address space can be demarcated into several areas. For example, the Modular One computer has three pairs of registers, and the three segments are used respectively for program, data private to a process, and data shared between processes. The disadvantages of this simple mechanism are that the number of segments is for economic reasons necessarily small, and that there needs to be a convention as to which segments are used for what purpose.

A more flexible arrangement of virtual memory is to allow the programmer to use a large number of segments according to his wishes, and to reference the segments by names assigned by himself. The address space thus becomes two-dimensional, since individual program addresses are identified by giving both a segment name and an address within the segment. (In fact for convenience of implementation the operating system replaces the segment name by a unique segment number when the segment is first referenced.) A generalised program address therefore consists of a pair $(s,a)$, where $s$ is the segment number and $a$ is the address within the segment.

*Figure 5.5 Simple address map for segmentation*

The address map can be implemented by means of a *segment table* for each process, the $s$th entry of which contains the base location and length of the $s$th segment of the process. The segment table entries are sometimes referred to as *segment descriptors*. In simplified form the mapping operation is (see figure 5.5)

(a)    Extract program address $(s,a)$
(b)    Use $s$ to index segment table
(c)    If $a < 0$ or $a > l$ then memory violation
(d)    $(b + a)$ is the required memory location

Protection against memory violation is provided by comparing the word address with the segment length $l$. Additional protection may be given by incorporating into each segment descriptor a number of *protection bits* (shown shaded in figure 5.5), which specify the modes in which the corresponding segment can be accessed. The programmer can then designate segments as being read only or execute only, and thus the sharing of segments between processes is possible without fear of corruption.

It is worth emphasising that despite the apparent similarity between figures 5.2 and 5.5 the address maps for paging and for segmentation are quite different in the following respects.

(a)   The purpose of segmentation is the logical division of address space; the purpose of paging is the physical division of memory to implement a one-level store.

(b)   Pages are of a fixed size determined by the machine architecture; segments can be of any size determined by the user (up to a limit fixed by the way in which the program address is partitioned into segment and word numbers).

(c)   The division of program address into page and word numbers is a function of the hardware, and overflow of the word number automatically increments the page number; the division into segment and word numbers is a logical one, and there is no overflow from word number to segment number. (If the word number overflows then a memory violation is generated.)

In practice the address mapping operation is not as simple as the foregoing description suggests. The major complication is that for large programs it may not be possible to hold all segments in main memory, particularly since the memory will be shared between several processes. This is effectively a situation in which the virtual memory is larger than the physical memory, and it can be treated either by employing paging or by swapping entire segments in and out of memory as required.

When paging is employed each segment generally consists of several pages and has its own page table. Provided that some of the segment's pages are in memory, the segment table entry points to the segment's page table; otherwise it is empty. The address mapping operation performed by the addressing hardware is as follows.

(a)   Extract program address $(s,a)$.
(b)   Use $s$ to index segment table.
(c)   If $s$th entry is empty then create a new (empty) page table, otherwise extract address of page table.
(d)   Split word address $a$ into page number $p$ and word number $w$.
(e)   Use $p$ to index page table.
(f)   If $p$th entry is empty then fetch page from backing store, otherwise extract page frame address $p'$.
(g)   Add $p'$ to word number $w$ to obtain required location.

Steps (a) to (c) represent the mapping due to segmentation; steps (d) to (g) (which correspond to figure 5.4) represent the mapping due to paging the segments.

The extra memory references required to access the segment and page tables can be avoided by the use of an associative store in a way similar to that described earlier for paging alone. In this case each entry in the associative store contains both the segment and page numbers of the most recently accessed pages. The segment and page bits of each program address are presented to the associative

store (figure 5.6) and if a match is found the word number is added to the corresponding page frame address to obtain the required memory location. Only when
no match is found is the full operation described above invoked.

If paging is not employed then segment table entries are as shown in figure 5.5.
A missing segment fault causes the whole of the required segment to be brought
into main memory; some other segment may have to be relegated to backing
store to create sufficient space. Policies for allocating memory among segments
will be described in the next section.

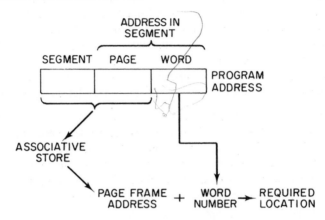

*Figure 5.6 Address mapping operation for paged*
*segments using associative store*

The advantages of using paging to implement a segmented address space are
twofold. Firstly, the entire segment need not be present in main memory — only
those pages currently in use need be accommodated; secondly, it is not necessary
that the pages occupy contiguous areas of memory — they can be dispersed
throughout memory wherever a suitable page frame is found. Against paging
must be set the complexity of the address map and the overhead of the page
tables. Examples of systems which have paged segments are the Honeywell 645,
ICL 2900 and the IBM 360/67; those which have unpaged segments are the large
Burroughs machines (for example, B6700) and the PDP-11/45.

## 5.4 MEMORY ALLOCATION POLICIES

The discussions in the last section were concerned exclusively with the *mechanisms*
of memory management rather than with the *policies* governing them. In this
section we shall concentrate on the policies which enable the mechanisms to be
put to good use.

Policies for managing memory fall into three broad categories.

(1)  *Replacement policies*, which determine what information is to be removed
from main memory, that is, create unallocated regions of memory.

(2) *Fetch policies*, which determine when information is to be loaded into main memory, for example on demand or in advance.

(3) *Placement policies*, which determine where information is to be placed in main memory, that is choose a subset of some unallocated region.

We shall see that policies of type (2) are very much the same for both paged and non-paged systems. Policies of types (1) and (3), however, differ between paged and non-paged systems: the differences arise from the fixed size of pages as opposed to the variable sizes of the blocks of information which have to be handled in non-paged systems.

## (1) Placement Policies for Non-paged Systems

In this subsection we are considering the transfer of information into main memory in the cases where the virtual address space is either segmented or implemented by base–limit pairs. In either case we shall denote the blocks of information which are being transferred by the word 'segment', with the understanding that if a single base–limit system is being used then a segment will be the entire address space of a process.

The situation is that from time to time segments are inserted into or deleted from the main memory. (The insertions and deletions occur on invocations of the fetch and replacement policies respectively.) If the system is in equilibrium, (that is, over a period of time the space freed by deletion is equal to that filled by insertion) then the memory has the chequer-board appearance of figure 5.7.

*Figure 5.7 Segmented memory*

It is clear that the placement policy must maintain a list of the locations and sizes of all unallocated 'holes'; we shall call this the *hole list*. Its task is to decide which hole to use, and to update the hole list after each insertion. If the segment to be placed is smaller than the hole to be used, then the segment is placed at the 'left-hand' or 'bottom end' of the hole. This tactic minimises the amount by which the hole is fragmented. If, on the other hand, the segment is larger than any available hole then the placement policy has the additional task of moving around the segments already in memory to create a hole large enough for its purpose.

Numerous placement algorithms are described in the literature, for example Knuth, (1968); we shall give four principal ones here. In each case the sizes of the holes are denoted by $x_1, x_2, ..., x_n$.

*(a) Best Fit*

The holes are listed in order of increasing size, that is $x_1 \leqslant x_2 \leqslant ... \leqslant x_n$. If $s$ is the size of the segment to be placed, then find the smallest $i$ such that $s \leqslant x_i$.

*(b) Worst Fit*

The holes are listed in order of decreasing size, that is $x_1 \geqslant x_2 \geqslant ... \geqslant x_n$. Place the segment in the first hole, and link the hole formed by the remaining space back into the appropriate position in the list.

*(c) First Fit*

The holes are listed in order of increasing base address. Find the smallest $i$ such that $s \leqslant x_i$. The use of the algorithm leads, after a time, to an accumulation of small holes near the head of the list. To avoid excessive search time for large segments the start position can be advanced cyclically by one element after each search.

*(d) Buddy*

For this algorithm segment sizes must be powers of 2, that is $s = 2^i$ for some $i$ less than a maximum $k$. A separate list is maintained for holes of each size $2^1$, $2^2$, ..., $2^k$. A hole may be removed from the $(i + 1)$-list by splitting it in half, thereby creating a pair of 'buddies' of size $2^i$ on the $i$-list. Conversely a pair of buddies may be removed from the $i$-list, coalesced, and put on the $(i + 1)$-list. The algorithm for finding a hole of size $2^i$ is recursive

```
procedure get hole (i);
begin if i = k + 1 then failure;
      if i-list empty then
      begin get hole (i + 1);
            split hole into buddies;
            put buddies on i-list
      end;
      take first hole in i-list
end
```

To the more suspicious reader it may appear strange that algorithms (a) and (b) are both viable since they adopt directly opposing strategies regarding the ordering of the hole list. Algorithm (a) is perhaps the more intuitively appealing since it appears to minimise the wastage in each hole it selects (that is, it selects the smallest hole that will do the job). Algorithm (b), however, works on the philosophy that making an allocation from a large hole is likely to leave a hole large enough to be useful in future, whereas making an allocation from a small hole will leave an even smaller hole which will probably be quite useless.

A problem common to all the placement policies described is *fragmentation* – the splitting up of free memory into holes so small that new segments cannot be fitted in. When this occurs some *compaction* of memory is necessary; that is, all segments must be moved downwards so that a single large hole appears at the top of memory. Compaction is most easily achieved if the holes are listed in address order, as in the first-fit algorithm. An alternative approach is to compact memory every time a segment is removed, thus avoiding fragmentation altogether; the overhead of frequent compaction is offset by not having to search a hole list whenever a segment is to be placed.

## (2) Placement Policies for Paged Systems

Placement policies for paged systems are far simpler than for non-paged systems; to place $k$ pages we simply use a replacement policy to free $k$ page frames. Fragmentation, in the sense described for non-paged systems, cannot occur, since all pages and page frames are of equal size. However, a paged system can suffer from a different form of fragmentation, *internal fragmentation*, which arises because the space required by a process is not usually an exact multiple of the page size. Consequently a part of the last page frame allocated is generally wasted: the average wastage can be expected to be half the page size. If the address space consists of several paged segments, the degree of internal fragmentation is multiplied by the number of segments currently held in main memory.

## (3) Replacement Policies for Paged Systems

The job of a replacement policy is to decide which blocks of information to relegate to secondary memory when space has to be found in main memory for new blocks. In this subsection we consider the case where the blocks of information are pages; we shall see later that the same policies can be applied, with appropriate modifications, in the non-paged situation.

Ideally one wants to replace the page which is not going to be referenced for the longest time in the future. Unfortunately, knowledge of the future is hard to come by: the best one can do is infer from past behaviour what future behaviour is likely to be. The accuracy of the inference depends on the predictability of program behaviour, which we shall discuss further in the section on fetch policies.

Three common replacement algorithms are

### (a) Least Recently Used (LRU)

'Replace the page which has least recently been used.' The assumption is that future behaviour will closely follow recent behaviour. The overhead is that of recording the sequence of access to all pages.

### *(b) Least Frequently Used (LFU)*

'Replace the page which has been used least frequently during some immediately preceding time interval.' The justification is similar to (a), and the overhead is that of keeping a 'use count' for each page. One drawback is that a recently loaded page will in general have a low use count and may be replaced inadvisedly. A way to avoid this is to inhibit the replacement of pages loaded within the last time interval.

### *(c) First-in First-out*

'Replace the page which has been resident longest.' This is a simpler algorithm, whose overhead is only that of recording the loading sequence of pages. It ignores the possibility that the oldest page may be the most heavily referenced.

Simulation studies (Colin, 1971) have shown a difference in performance of the three algorithms (in terms of the number of transfers required during the running of a number of jobs) which varies according to the type of jobs being run, but which is rarely more than fifteen per cent. Algorithm (c) gives a generally poorer performance than the other two.

Finally, it is worth noting that pages which have not been written to need not be transferred back to secondary memory provided a copy already exists there. A record of whether a particular page has been written to can be kept in a single bit in the corresponding page table entry.

### (4) Replacement Policies for Non-paged Systems

In this subsection we consider policies for the situation where the blocks of information to be replaced are segments in the broad sense defined in (1) above.

The major objective is the same as for paged systems — that is, to replace the segment which is least likely to be referenced in the immediate future. One might therefore expect the same policies to be applicable, and this is indeed the case, but with one major qualification. The qualification arises from the fact that not all segments occupy equal amounts of memory, so consideration of which segment to relegate to secondary memory is influenced by the size of the segment to be placed. If a small segment is to be brought into main memory then only a small segment need be replaced; on the other hand, the placement of a large segment requires the replacement of another large segment (or several smaller ones).

Possibly the simplest algorithm is to replace the single segment (if one exists) which, together with any adjacent holes, will free enough space for the incoming segment. If there are several such segments, then one of the policies discussed earlier, such as LRU, can be used to discriminate between them. If no single segment is large enough to create sufficient space, then several segments have to be replaced: a possible choice is the smallest set of contiguous segments which will free the space required.

The danger with such an algorithm is that the segment (or segments) replaced, being selected mainly on criteria of size, may be referenced again shortly afterwards. The danger can be reduced by selecting segments purely on an LRU (say) basis, but since the selected segments are not likely to be contiguous some compaction of memory will be required. The reader will readily appreciate that the relative emphasis given to segment size, expectation of future reference, and compaction, can produce a variety of complex algorithms which are difficult to assess except in practice. We shall not pursue the subject further here, but refer the interested reader to more detailed studies such as (Knuth, 1968) and (Denning, 1970).

## (5) Fetch Policies

Fetch policies determine when to move a block of information from secondary to main memory. The arguments for choosing a policy are roughly the same whether the blocks are pages or segments (in the broad sense we have been using). Fetch policies are divided into two broad classes: *demand* and *anticipatory*. Demand policies fetch blocks when they are needed; anticipatory policies fetch them in advance.

Demand policies are clearly the easier to implement — a missing block (segment or page) fault generates a fetch request, and the placement and/or replacement policies allocate memory for the new block. In non-paged systems (for example Burroughs machines) the transfer of blocks is usually on demand, as it is on some paged machines (for example Atlas).

Anticipatory policies rely on predictions of future program behaviour in order to be fully effective. Prediction can be based on two things

(a)    the nature of construction of programs
(b)    inference from a process's past behaviour

Consider (a) for a moment.

Many programs exhibit behaviour known as *operating in context*; that is, in any small time interval a program tends to operate within a particular logical module, drawing its instructions from a single procedure and its data from a single data area. Thus program references tend to be grouped into small localities of address space. The locality of reference is strengthened by the frequent occurrence of looping; the tighter the loop, the smaller the spread of references. The observation of this behaviour leads to the postulation (Denning, 1970) of the so called *principle of locality*: 'program references tend to be grouped into small localities of address space, and these localities tend to change only intermittently'

The validity of the principle of locality will vary from program to program; it will, for example, be more valid for programs making sequential array accesses than for programs accessing complex data structures. The principle is used by Denning in the context of paged memory to formulate the *working set* model of program behaviour which we briefly describe in the next section.

## 5.5 THE WORKING SET MODEL

The working set model of program behaviour (Denning, 1968) is an attempt to
establish a framework for understanding the performance of paging systems in a
multiprogramming environment. The policies for memory management which we
discussed in the last section are based on a study of how processes behave in
isolation; they do not take into account any effects which may arise from having
several processes in the machine at once. The competition for memory space
between processes can in fact lead to behaviour which would not occur if each
process ran separately.

As an illustration of what can happen, consider a single processor system with
a paged memory in which the degree of multiprogramming (that is, the number
of processes present in memory) is steadily increased. As the degree of multiprogramming rises one might expect that the processor utilisation would also
rise, since the dispatcher would always have a greater chance of finding a process
to run. Indeed observation confirms that this is generally the case, so long as the
degree of multiprogramming is kept below a certain level which is dependent on
the size of memory available. However, if the degree of multiprogramming exceeds
this level then it is found (see figure 5.8) that there is a marked increase in the
paging traffic between main and secondary memories accompanied by a sudden
decrease in processor utilisation. The explanation for this is that the high degree
of multiprogramming makes it impossible for every process to keep sufficient
pages in memory to avoid generating a large number of page faults. This means
that the backing store channel can become saturated, that most processes are
blocked awaiting a page transfer, and that the processor is under-utilised. This
state of affairs is referred to by the descriptive term *thrashing*.

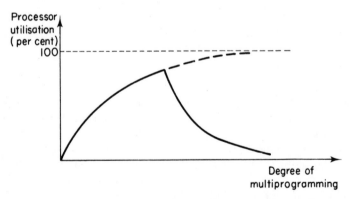

*Figure 5.8 Thrashing*

The lesson to be learned fron. this illustration is that each process requires a
certain minimum number of pages, called its *working set*, to be held in main
memory before it can effectively use the central processor. If less than this
number are present then the process is continually interrupted by page faults

which contribute towards thrashing. For thrashing to be avoided the degree of multiprogramming must be no greater than the level at which the working sets of all processes can be held in main memory.

The question now arises of how to determine which pages constitute the working set of a process. The answer is to inspect the process's recent history and to appeal to the principle of locality mentioned in the last section. More formally, the working set of a process at time $t$ is defined to be

$$w\,(t,h) = \left\{\text{page } i \mid \text{page } i \in N \text{ and page } i \text{ appears in the last } h \text{ references}\right\}$$

In other words the working set is the set of pages which have recently been referred to, 'recentness' being one of the parameters $(h)$ of the set. From the principle of locality one would expect the working set to change membership slowly in time. Denning has shown that the expected size $w\,(h)$ of the working set varies with $h$ as shown in figure 5.9.

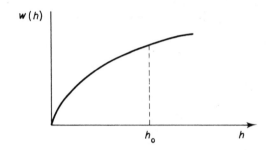

*Figure 5.9 Expected size of the working set*

As $h$ is increased (that is, the further into the past one looks), the fewer extra pages one expects to find in the working set. This enables one to establish a reasonably small value for $h$ (for example $h_0$) in the knowledge that a larger value of $h$ would not significantly increase the working set size.

As far as fetch and replacement policies are concerned the value of the working set lies in the following rule

'Run a process only if its entire working set is in main memory, and never remove a page which is part of the working set of some process.'

Although the working sets of some processes may be rather arbitrarily defined, and although the principle of locality does not apply to some programs, application of the above rule can make a significant contribution towards the prevention of thrashing. The working set model is used to govern paging on the Honeywell 645 in the MULTICS project, and hardware based on it has been implemented on the MANIAC II computer at the University of California.

It is important to realise that the rule given above is more than a pure memory management policy since it implies a correlation between memory allocation and processor allocation. So far in this chapter we have treated memory management as an issue distinct from the management of other resources. In practice management of a single resource cannot always be divorced from consideration of other resources, but we shall defer a full treatment of resource allocation until chapter 8.

## 5.6 IMPLEMENTATION IN THE PAPER SYSTEM

It may appear to the reader that the memory management policies discussed in this chapter have a rather *ad hoc* air, and that the choice of algorithm in a particular case is somewhat arbitrary. To a certain extent this is true; many of the policies are founded on common sense and experience, backed up in some cases by analytical or statistical justification. A powerful aid in the choice of algorithm is simulation; ideally each option should be tested with a simulation of the job mix expected. Some studies are reported by Knuth (1968), and an extensive bibliography is given by Denning (1970).

In order to implement in our paper operating system the mechanisms of section 5.3 we add to the volatile environment of each process

(1)     a copy of the contents of the base and limit registers
or (2)     a pointer to its segment table
or (3)     a pointer to its page table

depending on the architecture of our machine.

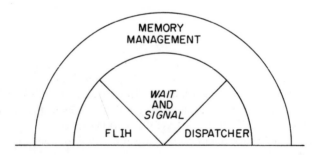

*Figure 5.10 Current state of the paper operating system*

If we have a non-paged machine then we introduce the hole list as a further data structure pointed to from the central table. The memory management layer of our system consists of code to implement the policies discussed in section 5.4.

Our system has now reached the stage shown in figure 5.10.

# 6 *Input and Output*

At this stage in the development of our paper operating system we have established an environment in which processes can exist and in which memory can be allocated to hold the associated programs and data. We now turn our attention to the means by which processes communicate with the outside world; that is, to mechanisms for the input and output of information.

Traditionally I/O is regarded as one of the more sordid areas of operating system design in that it is a field in which generalisation is difficult and *ad hoc* methods abound. The reason for this is the wide variety of peripheral devices employed; a particular configuration may include devices which differ greatly in their characteristics and mode of operation. Specifically, devices may differ on one or more of the following counts.

## (1) Speed

There may be a difference of several orders of magnitude between the data transfer rates of various devices. A magnetic drum, for instance, may be able to write $10^6$ characters per second, compared with a teletype speed of 10 characters per second.

## (2) Unit of Transfer

Data may be transferred in units of characters, words, bytes, blocks or records, according to the peripheral used.

## (3) Data Representation

An item of data may be encoded in different ways on different I/O media. Even on a single medium such as paper tape several different codes may be employed.

## (4) Permissible Operations

Devices differ in the kind of operation they can perform. One example is the obvious distinction between input and output; another is the ability to rewind magnetic tape but not a deck of cards.

**(5) Error Conditions**

Failure to complete a data transfer may have such various causes as a parity error, the end of a paper tape, a card wreck, or a checksum error, depending on the peripheral being used.

Clearly the diversity exemplified above is difficult to handle in a uniform manner. However we shall attempt in this chapter to construct a framework for an I/O system in which device-dependent characteristics are isolated as far as possible and in which some degree of uniformity is achieved. We start by considering some design objectives and their implications.

## 6.1 DESIGN OBJECTIVES AND IMPLICATIONS

### (1) Character Code Independence

It is obviously undesirable that in order to write his programs a user should require detailed knowledge of the character codes used by various peripherals. The I/O system must take responsibility for recognising different character codes and for presenting data to user programs in a standard form.

### (2) Device Independence

There are two aspects to device independence. First, a program should be independent of the particular device of a given type which it happens to be allocated. For example, it should not matter on which magnetic tape deck a particular tape is mounted, or which line printer is used for a program's output. Device independence of this kind ensures that a program does not fail simply because a particular device is broken or allocated elsewhere. It gives the operating system the freedom to allocated a device of the appropriate type according to overall availability at the time.

Second and more demanding, it is desirable that programs should as far as possible be independent of the device type used for their I/O. Clearly device independence of this nature cannot be carried as far as sending output to a card reader; what we have in mind is that only minimal changes to a job should be required for it to receive its data from cards rather than paper tape.

### (3) Efficiency

Since I/O operations often form a bottleneck in a computing system it is desirable to perform them as efficiently as possible.

### (4) Uniform Treatment of Devices

In the interests of simplicity and freedom from error it is desirable to handle all devices in a uniform manner. For reasons already mentioned this may be difficult in practice.

Some implications of these objectives are immediately apparent. First, character code independence implies the existence of a uniform internal representation of all characters. This representation is called the *internal character code*, and translation mechanisms must be associated with each peripheral to perform the appropriate conversions on input and output. For peripherals which may handle a variety of character codes a separate translation mechanism must be supplied for each code supported. Translation is performed immediately on input and immediately before output, so that only those processes intimately connected with peripheral handling need be aware of anything but the standard internal code. The translation mechanism will generally be a table, or in some cases a short piece of program.

Next, device independence implies that programs should operate not on actual devices but on virtual devices, variously called *streams* (Atlas), *files* (MULTICS), or *data sets* (IBM). The streams are used within a program without any reference to physical devices; the programmer merely directs output and input to or from particular streams. The association of streams with real devices is usally made by the operating system on the basis of information supplied by the user in the job description. We shall discuss job descriptions in detail in chapter 11; for our present purpose it is sufficient to say that the job description is a collection of user-supplied information, usually presented at the head of the job, which helps the operating system decide when and how to run it. A typical job description statement for the binding of a stream to a peripheral device is

$$\text{OUTPUT } 1 = \text{LPT}$$

meaning that output stream 1 is to be a line printer. Independence of a particular line printer is guaranteed by the operating system's freedom to associate the stream with any available printer; independence of device type is achieved by a trivial change to the job description (for example, paper tape output might be obtained by changing LPT to PTP).

*Figure 6.1 Device and stream information for a process*

The equivalence of streams and device types for a particular process can be recorded in a list of *stream descriptors* pointed to from its process descriptor (see figure 6.1); the allocation of a particular device of a given type is made when the process first uses the corresponding stream. We say that at this point the process *opens* the stream; the stream is *closed*, indicating that it is no longer to be used, either explicity by the process or implicity when the process terminates. For the process shown in figure 6.1, card reader 1 has been allocated as input stream 1, tape punch 3 has been allocated as output stream 2, and output stream 1, which has not yet been opened, is to be a line printer.

A third implication of our design objectives is that the I/O system should be constructed in such a way that device characteristics are clearly associated with the devices themselves rather than with the routines which handle them (the *device handlers*). In this way it is possible for device handlers to show great similarities, and for their differences of operation to derive solely from parametric information obtained from the characteristics of the particular device concerned. The necessary isolation of device characteristics can be achieved by encoding them in a *device descriptor* associated with each device, and by using the descriptor as a source of information for the device handler. The characteristic information about a device which may be stored in its desciptor is

(1)   the device identification
(2)   the instructions which operate the device
(3)   pointers to character translation tables
(4)   the current status: whether the device is busy, free, or broken
(5)   the current user process: a pointer to the process desciptor of the process, if any, which is currently using the device

All device descriptors can be linked together in a *device structure* which is pointed to from the central table.

## 6.2 THE I/O PROCEDURES

In the last section we made significant **progress** towards the uniform treatment of devices by isolating all device **dependent** characteristics in the device descriptors. We are now in a position to consider how the operating system handles a request for I/O from a user process.

A typical request from a process will be a call to the operating system of the general form

DOIO (*stream, mode, amount, destination, semaphore*)

where

| | |
|---|---|
| DOIO | is the name of a system *I/O procedure* |
| *stream* | is the number of the stream on which I/O is to take place |
| *mode* | indicates what operation, such as data transfers or rewind, is required; it may also indicate, if relevant, what character code is to be used |
| *amount* | is the amount of data to be transferred, if any |
| *destination* | (or source) is the location into which (or from which) the |

transfer, if any is to occur

*semaphore*      is the address of a semaphore *request serviced* which is to be
signalled when the I/O operation is complete

The I/O procedure DOIO is re-entrant, so that it may be used by several processes at once. Its function is to map the stream number to the appropriate physical device, to check the consistency of the parameters supplied to it, and to initiate service of the request.

The first of these operations is straightforward. The device which corresponds to the specified stream is determined from the information placed in the stream descriptor list of the calling process at the time the stream was opened (see figure 6.1). Once the device is identified the parameters of the I/O request can be checked for consistency against the information held in the device descriptor, and if an error is detected an exit can be made to the caller. One particular check which may be performed is that the device is capable of operating in the desired mode, another is that the size and destination of the data transfer correspond to the mode of operation. In the case of devices which can transfer only single characters the specified quantity of data to be transferred must be 1 and the destination either a register or memory location; for devices which transfer blocks of data directly to memory the specified quantity must be equal to the block size (fixed or variable according to the device) and the destination the memory location at which the transfer is to start.

When the checks have been completed the I/O procedure assembles the parameters of the request into an *I/O request block* (IORB) which it adds to a queue of similar blocks which represent other requests for use of the same device. These other requests may come from the same process, or, in the case of a shared device such as a disc, from other processes. The *device request queue* is attached to the descriptor of the device concerned (see figure 6.2), and is serviced by a separate process called a *device handler* which we shall describe in the next section. The I/O procedure notifies the device handler that it has placed a request on the queue by signalling a semaphore *request pending* associated with the device and which is contained in the device descriptor. Similarly, once the I/O operation is complete the device handler notifies the user process by means of the semaphore *request serviced* whose address was a parameter of the I/O procedure and was passed to the device handler as an element of the IORB. This semaphore can be initialised either by the user process or by the I/O procedure when the IORB is created.

The complete I/O routine is

```
procedure DOIO (stream, mode, amount, destination, semaphore);
begin  lookup device in process descriptor;
       check parameters against device characteristics;
       if error then error exit;
       assemble IORB;
       add IORB to device request queue;
       signal (request pending)
end;
```

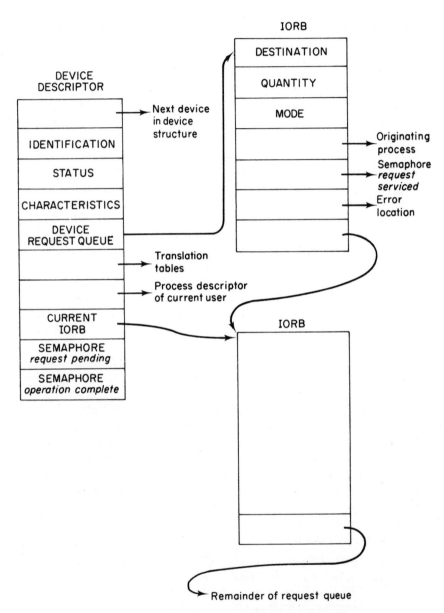

*Figure 6.2 Device descriptor and device request queue*

## 6.3 THE DEVICE HANDLERS

As mentioned in the last section a device handler is a process which is responsible for servicing the requests on a device request queue and for notifying the originating process when the service has been completed. There is a separate handler for each device, but since all handlers operate in a similar way they can make use of shareable programs. Any differences in behaviour between handlers are derived from the characteristics stored in the descriptors of the particular devices.

A device handler operates in a continuous cycle during which it removes an IORB from the request queue, initiates the corresponding I/O operation, waits for the operation to be completed, and notifies the originating process. The complete cycle for an input operation is

```
repeat indefinitely
begin   wait (request pending);
        pick an IORB from request queue;
        extract details of request;
        initiate I/O operation;
        wait (operation complete);
        if error then plant error information;
        translate character(s) if necessary;
        transfer data to destination;
        signal (request serviced);
        delete IORB
end;
```

The following notes, which should be read with reference to figure 6.2, may clarify the details.

(1)   The semaphore *request pending*, contained in the device descriptor, is signalled by the I/O procedure each time it places an IORB on the request queue for this device. If the queue is empty the semaphore is zero and the device handler is suspended.

(2)   The device handler may pick an IORB from the queue according to any desired priority algorithm. A first come, first served algorithm is usually adequate, but the handler could be influenced by priority information placed in the IORB by the I/O procedure. In the case of a disc the device handler may service requests in an order which minimises head movements.

(3)   The instructions to initiate the I/O operation can be extracted from the device characteristics held in the device desciptor.

(4)   The semaphore *operation complete* is signalled by the interrupt routine after an interrupt is generated for this device. The outline program of the interrupt routine, which is entered from the first-level interrupt handler, is

```
locate device descriptor;
signal (operation complete);
```

The semaphore *operation complete* is held in the device descriptor. Note that the interrupt routine is very short; all housekeeping is performed by the device handler, which operates in user mode as a normal process.

(5)   The error check is made by interrogating the device status when the operation is complete. If there has been an error, such as parity or card wreck, or even end of file, information about it is deposited in an *error location* whose address is included by the I/O procedure in the IORB.

(6)   Character translation is made according to the mode specified in the IORB and the tables pointed at from the device descriptor.

(7)   The cycle shown above is for an input operation. In the case of an output operation the extraction of data from its source and any character translation occurs before the operation rather than after.

(8)   The address of the semaphore *request serviced* is passed to the device handler as a component of the IORB. It is supplied by the process requesting I/O as a parameter of the I/O procedure.

The synchronisation and flow of control between the process requesting I/O, the I/O procedure, and the appropriate device handler and interrupt routine are summarised in figure 6.3. Solid arrows represent transfers of control; broken arrows represent synchronisation by means of semaphores. It is important to note that in the scheme illustrated the requesting process proceeds asynchronously with the device handler so that it may perform other computations or make other I/O requests while the original request is being serviced. The requesting process need be held up only on occasions when the I/O operation is incomplete when it executes *wait* (*request serviced*).

*Figure 6.3 Sketch of the I/O system*

The disadvantage of this arrangement is that the requesting process must take responsibility for synchronising its activities with those of the device handler. It must not, for example, attempt to use input data which has not yet been provided. This means that the author of the process must be aware that I/O operations are not instantaneous and must be capable of achieving the desired synchronisation by appropriate use of the semaphore *request serviced*.

An alternative arrangement is to place the responsibility for synchronisation within the I/O procedure, which is part of the operating system. This can be done by making the semaphore *request serviced* local to the I/O procedure (that is, its address need no longer be supplied by the requesting process) and by inserting the operations

*wait* (*request serviced*);

test error location;

in the I/O procedure immediately before its exit. The delay implicit in an I/O operation is now hidden within the operating system; as far as the requesting process is concerned the operation is instantaneous in the sense that when the next instruction after the request is obeyed the operation can be assumed complete. To put it another way, the requesting process is executing on a virtual machine in which I/O operations are achieved by a single instantaneous instruction.

The two possible arrangements discussed above may be summarised as follows. In the first the user has the freedom to continue in parallel with the I/O operation but has the responsibility of detecting its completion; in the second the responsibility is taken away from him but he also loses the freedom.

## 6.4 BUFFERING

The description of the I/O procedure and the device handlers given above assumes that all data transfers are unbuffered. That is, each I/O request from a process causes a physical transfer to occur on the appropriate peripheral. If the process is performing repeated transfers on the same stream it will repeatedly be suspended (on *wait* (*request serviced*)) while the transfers take place. In order to avoid heavy overheads in process switching it is sometimes convenient to perform I/O transfers in advance of requests being made, thus ensuring that data is available when required. This technique is known as *buffering*.

Input transfers are made by the operating system into an area of memory called an input buffer; the user process takes its data from the buffer and is forced to wait only when the buffer becomes empty. When this occurs the operating system refills the buffer and the process continues. Similarly, ouput transfers from a process are directed to an output buffer, and the operating system empties the entire buffer when it is full. The process has to wait only if it tries to output an item before the system has emptied the buffer.

The technique can be refined by the use of two buffers rather than one: so called *double buffering*. A process now transfers data to (or from) one buffer while the operating system empties (or fills) the other. This ensures that the process will wait only if both buffers are filled (or exhausted) before the operating system has taken action. This will happen only when the process performs a rapid burst of I/O, and in this case the problem can often be solved by the addition of yet more buffers (*multiple buffering*). Of course no amount of buffering can help those cases in which a process demands I/O at a rate which is consistently higher than that at which the I/O devices can work. The usefulness of buffering is restricted to smoothing out peaks in I/O demand in situations where the *average* demand is no greater than the I/O devices can service. In general, the higher the peaks the greater is the number of buffers required to achieve the smoothing.

Whether or not a stream is to be buffered may be declared by an appropriate statement in the job description; in the buffered case the user may specify how many buffers are to be used or allow the system to supply a default value, usually two. The operating system allocates space for buffers when the stream is opened, and records the buffer address in the stream descriptor.

A slightly different I/O procedure is needed to allow for buffered operation. The new procedure handles an input request by extracting the next item from the appropriate buffer and passing it directly to the calling process. Only when a buffer becomes empty does the procedure generate an IORB and signal to the device handler to supply more input. When the stream is opened the I/O procedure generates enough IORBs to fill all the buffers. The device handler operates as before, initiating a data transfer into the buffer whose location is indicated in the IORB. Similar remarks apply, *mutatis mutandis*, to output requests. In both cases the I/O procedure and the device handler together form a variation of the producer–consumer pair described in chapter 3.

The I/O procedure for buffered operations can be called from a user process by a statement of the general form

DOBUFFIO (*stream, mode, destination*)

where *stream, mode,* and *destination* are as described for procedure DOIO in section 6.2. The amount of information transferred will be a single item. Note that since any delays arising from full or empty buffers are hidden in the I/O procedure there is no need to pass a semaphore address as one of the parameters. The type of buffering, if any, the addresses of the buffers, and the semaphores to be used by the I/O procedures are all accessible from the stream descriptor list of the calling process (see figure 6.4b). The first element of this information can be used to determine which I/O procedure to call to effect a transfer.

## 6.5 FILE DEVICES

In the foregoing discussion we have implicitly assumed that the name of a peripheral device is sufficient information to determine the external source or destination of a given transfer. This is true of peripherals which operate sequentially, so that there is no ambiguity about what area of the external medium a data transfer is directed to or from. A paper tape reader, for example, can read only the next character on the tape, while a line printer can print only on the current line. In some cases it may be possible to advance the medium by a certain amount (to a new page, say), but there is no question of being able to direct a transfer to any part of the medium at will. Other devices, such as disc drives and drums, which operate in a random access mode, provide the facility of selecting a particular area of the medium (disc or drum) on which to effect the transfer. In these cases it is not sufficient to name the device involved; it is also necessary to specify what data area on the medium is to be used.

Each data area which can exist on such media is called a *file*, and usually has an arbitrary size which is defined when it is created or updated. A device which supports files is called a *file device*. We shall say more in the next chapter about the organisation of files; for the moment we shall assume that each file has a unique name which can be used by the operating system to determine the location of the file on the appropriate medium. A directory of file names and the corresponding locations is kept by the operating system for this purpose.

*Figure 6.4 Stream information for file and non-file devices (T = device type)*

When a data stream is to be directed to or from a file device the stream is associated in the job description with the name of a particular file rather than with the name of the device. A typical job description statement might be

INPUT 1 = 'TESTDATA'

indicating that data on stream 1 is to come from the file named TESTDATA. When the stream is opened the operating system looks up the file name in the directory, to find the particular device and location where the file is stored. This procedure, known as *opening* the file, includes various checks which will be detailed in the next chapter; because it can be a lengthy operation it is not desirable to repeat it for each data transfer. Consequently each time a file is opened a *file descriptor* is created to hold the information which will be required for forthcoming transfers. This information includes the address of the device descriptor of the device on which the file is stored, the location of the file on that device, whether the file is to be written to or read from, and details of the file's internal organisation. A pointer to the file descriptor is placed in the appropriate stream descriptor of the process opening the file, as illustrated in figure 6.4a. The reader will see from a comparison of figures 6.4a and 6.4b that the file descriptor adds extra information to the association of streams with physical devices. The I/O procedures, which perform the association for each data transfer, can readily be modified to take this information into account when assembling an IORB.

## 6.6 SPOOLING

The preceding sections have made an implicit distinction between shareable devices, such as disc drives, which can handle successive requests from different processes, and unshareable devices, such as line printers, which can necessarily be allocated to only one process at a time. The unshareable devices are those which operate in such a way that their allocation to several processes at once would lead to an inextricable intermingling to I/O transactions. As pointed out in section 6.1, the allocation of an unshareable device is made when a process opens a stream associated with it; the device is released only when the stream is closed or the process terminates. Processes which wish to use a device when it is already allocated must wait for it to be released. This implies that during periods of high demand several processes may be held up waiting for the use of scarce devices, while during other periods these same devices may be lying unused. In order to spread the load and reduce the possibility of bottlenecks some other strategy may be needed.

The solution adopted by many systems is to *spool* all I/O for heavily used devices. This means that instead of performing a transfer directly on the device associated with a stream the I/O procedures execute the transfer on some intermediate medium, usually disc. The responsibility of moving data between the disc and the required device is vested in a separate process, called a *spooler*, which is associated with that device. As an example, consider a system in which all line printer output is spooled. Each process which opens a line printer stream is allocated an anonymous file on disc, and all output on the stream is directed to this file by the I/O procedure. The file is in effect acting as a virtual line printer. When the stream is closed the file is added to a queue of similar files created by other processes, all of which are waiting to be printed. The function of the line printer spooler is to take files from the queue and send them to the printer. It is assumed, of course, that over a period of time the speed of the printer is adequate to handle all the output files generated. A skeletal structure for the spooler is

```
repeat indefinitely
begin  wait (something to spool);
       pick file from queue;
       open file;
       repeat until end of file
       begin DOIO (parameters for disc read);
             wait (disc request serviced);
             DOIO (parameters for line printer output);
             wait (printer request serviced)
       end
end;
```

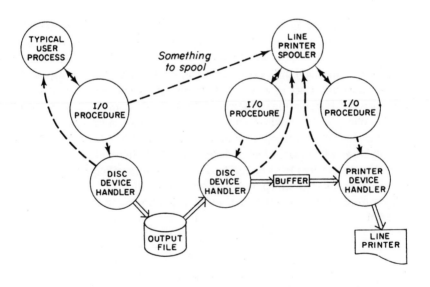

*Figure 6.5 Output spooling*

The reader may note the following points.

(1)   The structure will in practice be modified to allow for buffering the data between disc and printer.
(2)   The semaphore *something to spool* is signalled by any process which closes a line printer stream (that is, completes an output file).
(3)   The output queue need not be processed on a first come, first served basis; the spooler may for example favour short files over long ones.

The relationships between the spooler, the device handlers, and the processes producing the output are summarised in figure 6.5. A similar diagram, based on an analogous discussion to the above, could be drawn for an input spooler.

In summary we can say that spooling evens out the pressure of demand on heavily used peripherals. As we shall see in chapter 8 it also reduces the possibility of deadlock arising from injudicious peripheral allocation. A further advantage is that it is relatively easy to produce several copies of the same output without rerunning the job. On the debit side are the large amounts of disc space needed to hold the input and output queues, and the heavy traffic on the disc channel. Finally, spooling is of course not feasible in a real-time environment since I/O transactions are required immediately.

### 6.7 CONCLUSIONS

In the preceding sections we have outlined an I/O system which satisfies the objectives of character code independence, device independence, and the uniform treatment of devices. These qualities have been gained at the expense of efficiency; the I/O procedures and device handlers we presented will, because of their generalised nature, work more slowly than specialised pieces of code tailor-made for particular I/O operations or devices. However, the framework we have laid down is conceptually sound, and may be used as a basis for optimisation. The greatest gains would in practice come from replacing the code of the I/O procedures and device handlers, which is driven by information in I/O requests and device descriptors, by pieces of device and operation specific program. This would of course blur the uniform approach we have established.

The current stage of development of the paper operating system is shown in figure 6.6.

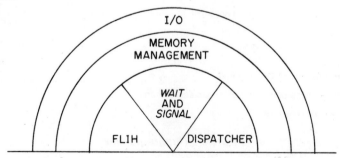

*Figure 6.6 Current state of the paper operating system*

# 7 *The Filing System*

## 7.1 OBJECTIVES

It was mentioned in chapter 2 that the facility for long-term storage is a desirable
characteristic of an operating system. The motivation for long-term storage varies
according to the nature of the system, but generally derives from consideration
of one or both of the following benefits.

### (1) On-line Storage

For certain applications concerned with information retrieval (such as management
information systems) it is necessary to store large quantities of data in such a way
that they are always accessible. Even in those areas such as job-shop systems where
a large on-line data base is not essential, it is a great convenience to the user to be
able to store programs or data within the computing system itself rather than on
some external medium such as punched cards. In multi-access systems in particular
it is impracticable to expect the user to manage without on-line storage, since the
only I/O device at his disposal is the terminal on which he types. Few users would
tolerate a system in which all their programs and data had to be typed in afresh
at the start of every session on the terminal. Even in batch systems on-line
storage of information can increase throughput by reducing dependency on slow
peripherals.

### (2) Sharing of Information

In some systems it is desirable that users should be able to share information. For
example, the users of a job-shop system may wish to use each other's programs
or data, and in a transaction processing system many separate processes may use
the same data base. In the job-shop case it may even be desirable for the installation to provide a set of *library* programs, such as editors, compilers, or scientific
subroutines, which are commonly available to its users. If information is to be
shared in this way then it must be stored on-line over long periods of time.

   For reasons of economy long-term storage is effected on secondary media
such as discs, drums and magnetic tapes, and it is the purpose of the *filing system*
to provide the means of organising and accessing the data in a way convenient to

the user. The way this is done will naturally depend on the kind of data and the uses to which it is to be put; the filing system for a transaction processing system can be expected to be quite different from that for a job-shop system. In this chapter we shall keep to the spirit of the book in confining ourselves to job-shop systems, in which the filing systems are generally disc based; the reader who is interested in other areas is referred to the extensive literature elsewhere (for example IFIP, 1969; Judd, 1973; Martin, 1977).

The user of a job-shop system arranges his data in *files* of arbitrary size. Each file is thus a collection of data which is regarded as an entity by the user; it may be a program, a set of procedures, or the results of an experiment. The file is the logical unit which is stored and manipulated by the filing system. The medium on which files are stored is usually divided into *blocks* of fixed length (typically 128 to 512 words), and the filing system must allocate the appropriate number of blocks to each file. In order to be useful the filing system must

(1)    Allow creation and deletion of files.
(2)    Allow access to files for reading or writing.
(3)    Perform automatic management of secondary memory space. It should be of no concern to the user whereabouts his files are located in secondary memory.
(4)    Allow reference to files by symbolic name. Since the user does not know, nor wish to know, the physical location of his files, he should be required only to quote their names in order to refer to them.
(5)    Protect files against system failure. Users will be reluctant to commit themselves to the system unless convinced of its integrity.
(6)    Allow the sharing of files between co-operating users but protect files against access by unauthorised users.

In the following sections we examine how the above objectives can be achieved.


## 7.2 FILE DIRECTORIES AND FILE STORAGE

The basic problem in accessing a file is to map a symbolic file name to a physical location in secondary memory. The mapping is achieved by means of a *file directory*, or *catalogue*, which is basically a table containing information about the locations of named files. Since the directory is the mechanism through which the file is accessed it is natural to include in it some means of protection against unauthorised access. We shall discuss this further in the next section; for the present we observe that an immediate measure of security can be afforded by dividing the directory into two levels as shown in figure 7.1. At the upper level a *master file directory* (MFD) contains for each user in the system a pointer to a *user file directory* (UFD) for that user; at the lower level each UFD contains the names and locations of a single user's files. Since a UFD can be accessed only via the MFD the privacy of a user's files can be assured by a simple identity check at the MFD level. Moreover, it is possible for different users to use the same name for a file without confusion, since the *full name* of a file can be regarded as the concatenation of the user name (or number) with the *individual name* of the file. For example, the individual name of the file shown in figure 7.1 is PROG, and its full name is FRED.PROG. Another file with the same individual name, but belonging to a user BILL, would have full name BILL.PROG. In practice it is not always necessary to specify the full name of a file, since the filing system can use the identity of the person requesting access as the default value for the first component. Only when a user requests access to another user's file does he need to quote the name in full.

*Figure 7.1 Two-level directory structure*

The information in each UFD entry generally consists of

(1)   The file name.
(2)   The physical location of the file in secondary memory.
(3)   The file type (character, binary, relocatable, etc.). This information is kept largely for user convenience, and also for the convenience of systems programs, such as loaders or editors, which may be used to operate on the file. As far as the filing system itself is concerned each file is simply a string of bits.
(4)   Access control information (for example read only; see section 7.4).
(5)   Administrative information (for example time of last update). This information is used to provide data for the system activities of preserving duplicate copies as insurance against hardware failure (see section 7.5).

The form of the entry indicating the physical location of the file will vary according to the way in which the file is stored. The arbitrary size of a file, and the fact that it may change in length when it is updated, imply that the blocks in which it is stored must be chained in some way. This may be done in several ways, three of which we describe below.

### (1) Block Linkage

One word in each block of the file is used as a pointer to the next block (see figure 7.2). The UFD entry for the file points to the first block in the chain. The space overhead involved is one word per block for each file.

A disadvantage of this method of chaining is the large number of disc accesses which are needed to find the end of the file. This can be particularly inconvenient if the file is to be deleted and the space occupied returned to a free list (see section 7.4); the alterations to pointers which are required to return the space rely on a knowledge of the position of the end of the file. For this reason the UFD entry is often extended to point to the last block in the file as well as to the first.

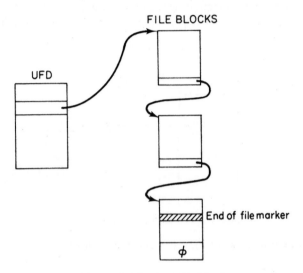

*Figure 7.2 Linked file blocks*

The reader will note that access to the file is necessarily sequential since all blocks can be reached only by passing down the chain. This method of chaining is therefore best suited to situations in which the files are processed sequentially. In these cases the overhead in accessing the file is only that of reading the successive blocks.

### (2) File Map

For this method of file linkage the state of the disc is recorded in a *file map* in which each disc block is represented by a single word. The UFD entry for a file points to the location in the file map which represents the first block in the file. This location in turn points to the location in the map which represents the next block in the file, and so on (see figure 7.3). The last block in the file is represented by a null pointer. Thus the file shown in figure 7.3 occupies blocks 3,6,4 and 8 of the disc. The space overhead of the method is one word for every disc block.

As with the block linkage method access to the file is necessarily sequential. As an aid to extending and deleting a file the UFD entry may contain a pointer to the location in the file map which represents the file's last block.

Since the file map is generally too large to be held in main memory it must be stored on disc as a file itself and brought into memory a block at a time as required. This means that to read a file of $N$ blocks may require an extra $N$ disc accesses to read the appropriate parts of the file map. The overhead will be less than this only if some of the locations representing successive blocks of the file happen to lie in the same block of the file map. For this reason it is clearly advantageous to keep the space occupied by each file as near contiguous as possible, rather than allowing the file to be spread over the entire disc.

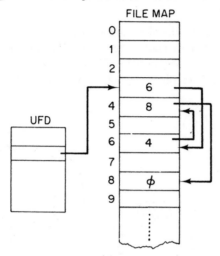

*Figure 7.3 File map*

## (3) Index Blocks

The linkage pointers for each file are stored in a separate *index block* on disc. If the file is large then several index blocks may be needed, each one chained to the next (see figure 7.4). The UFD entry for the file points to the first index block in the chain. Since the last index block for a file is unlikely to be fully used the average space overhead is slightly more than one word per block for each file. The overhead for small files is proportionately greater than for large ones.

The great advantage of index blocks is that the file need not be accessed sequentially; any block may be accessed at random simply by specifying the name of the file and an offset in the index block. This method of file storage therefore lends itself to situations in which files possess an internal structure and in which the individual components are to be accessed separately.

The time overhead in accessing the file is small: the first access requires the index block to be read, but subsequent accesses carry no overhead unless different index blocks are needed. However, the addition or deletion of blocks in the middle of the file implies a rearrangement of pointers in the index blocks. This can be a lengthy operation and means that this method of storage is unsuitable for files which change frequently.

We remark in passing that in each of the above methods the end of each file can be denoted by a special marker at the appropriate place in the last block. This can be done for any type of file for which a unique marker can be defined which cannot be interpreted as data. For example, the end of file marker for character files could be a bit pattern which does not represent any known characters. However, no such marker can be defined for binary files since all bit patterns form valid data. In this case it is necessary to record the length of a file (in words or bytes) as an extra component of its UFD entry. (This is probably a good idea in any case, since it can give an extra check against corruption of a file.)

As a final observation on file block linkage we remark that a system may allow several forms of linkage, particularly where some files are likely to be accessed sequentially and others non-sequentially. The type of linkage required may be specified by the user when a file is created, with a suitable default being supplied by the system.

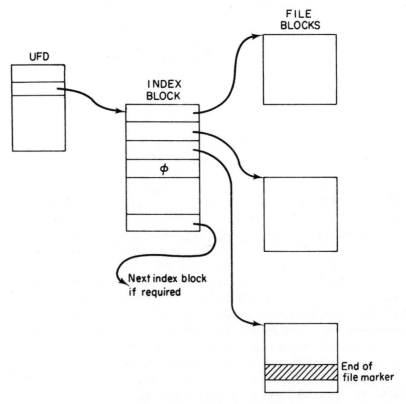

*Figure 7.4 Use of index blocks*

Many systems (for example the DEC System-10) adopt the two-level directory structure described earlier. Others, such as GEORGE 3, extend the concept to a multi-level structure, in which directory entries may be pointers to either files or other directories (see figure 7.5). A multi-level structure is useful in situations where the stored information has a tree-like classification, or where the users are grouped in hierarchies such as individuals within project teams within departments. In the latter case a hierarchical protection mechanism can be applied by making increasingly stringent checks as one progresses further down the tree. As in the two-level system, conflicting file names can be resolved by regarding the full name of the file as the concatenation of its individual name with the names of the directories on its access path.

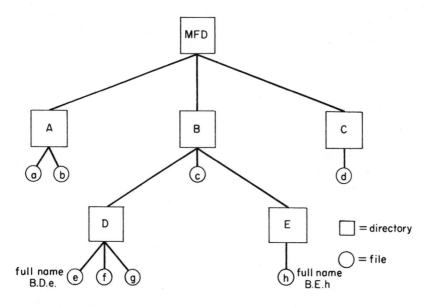

*Figure 7.5 Multi-level directory structure*

The disadvantage of a multi-level system lies in the length of the path to any particular file and the number of disc accesses which must be made to follow the path through the various directories. This can be alleviated to some extent by making use of the tendency of successive file accesses to be directed to files in the same directory. Once a route is established through the tree structure to a particular directory then this directory can be designated the *current directory* and subsequent file references need quote only the individual file name. A change of current directory is made by quoting the file name in full. This technique is used in GEORGE 3 and in MULTICS (Daley and Neumann, 1965).

## 7.3 SHARING AND SECURITY

The problem of the security of files arises directly from the desire to share them.

In a non-sharing environment, where the only person allowed to access a file is the owner himself, security can be achieved by making an identity check in the MFD. When files are to be shared, however, the owner requires a means of specifying which users are to be allowed access to his files, and which are not. Moreover it is convenient for the owner to be able to specify *what kind* of access is to be permitted; he may wish some of his friends to be able to update his files, others only to read them, and others merely to load them for execution. We may summarise this by saying that the owner must be able to specify what *access privileges* other users may have.

A particularly simple way of doing this is to associate with each file a set of access privileges applicable to various classes of user. The user classes might be

(1)   the owner
(2)   partners
(3)   others

and typical access privileges are

(1)   no access (N)
(2)   execute only (E)
(3)   read only (R)
(4)   append only (A)
(5)   update (U)
(6)   change protection (P)
(7)   delete (D)

Each access privilege generally implies the ones above it. A typical *file protection key* assigned by the owner when creating the file, would be DAR, meaning that the owner can do anything, partners can append, and anyone else can only read. The file protection key resides in the owner's UFD as part of the entry for that particular file. Note that in some cases it may be sensible for the owner to grant himself only a low access privilege in order to protect himself from his own mistakes. Despite this the filing system must always allow the owner the change protection privilege, since otherwise he would have no way of altering or deleting his own file.

An implication of this method is that the owner must list in his UFD those users who are designated partners, and this list must be checked for all accesses other than by the owner himself. In some systems it is possible to avoid this by defining partnerships implicitly: the identification by which the user is known to the system may be structured so that its first component indicates partnership and its second component the individual user identity. For example, on the DEC System-10 the user identification consists of the pair (*project number, user number*), and all users with the same project number are deemed to be partners as far as file access is concerned. This technique is clearly inadequate when different but overlapping partnerships are required for different files.

The user class method of protection was initially developed in the mid-1960s for the Atlas 2, which had seven different access privileges and four classes of user (partnerships were defined explicitly by the user); it is now employed in several systems, such as the DEC System-10, which has eight access privileges and three classes of user (partnerships are defined implicitly).

A more general technique, which overcomes the hierarchical limitations of user classes, is for the owner to list in his UFD all users to whom he has accorded access privileges, together with a specification of what the privileges are. If a single list is associated with the entire UFD then the privileges accorded are necessarily the same for all files; alternatively, separate lists may be associated with each UFD entry, so that different privileges may be given to different sets of users for different files. In the latter case a great deal of space may be taken up by the lists, and unless the increased flexibility is essential this method should probably not be used.

A variation of this technique, used in MULTICS (Daley and Neumann, 1965), is for the owner to allow other users to create links in their UFDs to entries within his own UFD. Figure 7.6 shows a user Fred who has a link to a file entry in another user Jim's UFD. The link allows Fred to access the corresponding file belonging to Jim. Jim's UFD will contain a list of all users whom he allows to make such links. The great disadvantage of this method is that when a file is deleted all links to it must also be deleted, which means that the system must have a way of finding where all the links are.

*Figure 7.6 Links between UFDs*

Summarising, the techniques described above offer various solutions to the problem of sharing and security. In general the more flexible the method adopted the greater is the space overhead in the UFDs and the longer the time to perform an access.

## 7.4 SECONDARY MEMORY ORGANISATION

As mentioned in section 7.1 file storage space is generally allocated in fixed size blocks, and since file sizes are variable, some kind of dynamic storage technique is required to allocate blocks to files and keep track of free space. One method is to regard free blocks as constituting a file in their own right, and to link them by one of the techniques described in section 7.2. If the index block technique is used then all operations on the free chain (that is, allocating and returning free blocks) must take place at its tail since operations at the head would involve the rearrangement of a large number of pointers. If the block linkage or file map technique is used the operations may take place at either end of the chain. The index block technique has the further disadvantage that when $N$ blocks are allocated or returned then $N$ pointers must be deleted from or inserted in the last index block. By contrast only two pointers need changing when the other two techniques are used, no matter how many blocks are allocated or returned. (For example, when blocks are returned to the end of the free chain the two pointers which need changing are one from the last block of the old chain to the first block of the addition, and one from the system directory to the end of the new chain.)

A different method of recording free space is to use a *bit map*, which is an area of memory in which each bit represents a disc block. If a block is free the corresponding bit is set to zero; if the block is being used the bit is set to one. In order to find $N$ free blocks it is necessary only to search the bit map for the first $N$ zero bits, and then perform a simple calculation to obtain the corresponding block addresses.

In some situations the bit map may be too large to be held conveniently in main memory. In these cases the map can be stored in secondary memory, with only a section of it in main memory. This section can be used for all allocations, and when it is full (that is, all bits are one) it can be swapped for another section. The return of free space involves retrieving that section of the map corresponding to the returned blocks, and setting the appropriate bits to zero. This may result in heavy traffic of the disc map, but this can be reduced by keeping a list of all returned blocks and using it to update the map each time a new section of it comes into main memory. This technique must be applied with care, so that in the event of a disc crash the state of the bit map remains consistent with the space allocated.

The choice of block size is generally made by the hardware designer (a notable exception being the IBM 360 and 370 series, where the user may make a separate choice for each file). The choice is made according to the following criteria.

(1)   The waste of space due to some blocks not being filled. This will increase as the block size increases.
(2)   The waste of space due to chain pointers. The smaller the blocks the more pointers are required.
(3)   The unit in which the storage device transfers data to main memory. The

block size should be a multiple of this unit so as to fully utilise each data transfer.

(4) The amount of memory needed for each read or write operation on a file. Depending on the method of disc organisation, space may have to be found in memory for the current index block or the current file map block, as well as for the block being read or written.

Typical block sizes are 128, 256, or 512 words.

Space allocation strategies can range from the straightforward (use the first block on the free block chain or the first block in the bit map) to the sophisticated (use the block which will minimise the amount of disc head movement when reading the file). The overhead of seek time in reading a file whose blocks are scattered all over the disc can in fact be quite large and can lead to saturation of the disc channel. It can be reduced by the strategy outlined above, or by periodically going through the file structure concatenating files as much as possible. This latter technique can be built into the back-up procedures described in the next section.

## 7.5 FILE SYSTEM INTEGRITY

Since the content of files may represent many months' work or may consist of irreplaceable data it is essential that a filing system provides adequate mechanisms for back-up and recovery in the not unlikely event of hardware or software failure. This means that the system must maintain duplicate copies of all files so that they can be restored after any unfortunate occurrence.

There are two principal ways of making copies of files, the first and simpler of which is known as the *periodic* (or *massive*) *dump*. At fixed intervals of time the contents of the entire file store are dumped onto some medium, usually magnetic tape, and in the event of failure all files can be recreated in the state they were in when the last dump was taken. Single files which are inadvertently deleted may be retrieved at the expense of scanning the entire dump tape. The disadvantages of the periodic dump are

(1) The file system may have to be placed out of use during the period of the dump. The alternative is not to dump any files which are open for writing.
(2) The dump usually takes a long time (20 minutes to 2 hours, depending on the size of the system and the speed of the tape decks). This means that the dump cannot be performed very often, and so a retrieved file may well be out of date.

The second and more sophisticated technique is the *incremental dump* (Fraser, 1969). With this technique a dump is made only of that information which has been changed since the previous dump was taken. This means that only files which have been created or altered, and directory entries which have been modified, will be dumped on each occasion. The amount of such information will be small, and so the dump can be made at frequent intervals. In order to determine which files are to be dumped a flag in the directory entry of each file is set whenever the file is altered, and cleared when it is dumped. So that the dumping process does not have to examine all directory entries, a global flag in each UFD can be used to indicate whether any individual flags within the UFD are set. Since the dumping process will skip all files whose flags are not set, which includes all files which are currently being updated, it can run in parallel with normal work. It is even possible, as in MULTICS, for the dumper to be a low priority process which is always present in the machine and which continually searches directories looking for updated information.

The disadvantages of the incremental dump lie in the large quantities of data which are generated and in the complexity of the recovery procedure. After a failure information must be reconstructed from the sequence of events recorded on the dump tapes. The tapes are mounted in inverse chronological order, and the filing system is restored back to the time that the last periodic dump was taken. (Periodic dumps will be made at rare intervals, typically once a week.) During this procedure the reloading process picks out from the dump tapes only those files it has not already restored, so that recent files are not superseded by earlier versions. Finally the last periodic dump tape is used to complete the recovery operation. This method of procedure is superior to starting with the periodic dump tape and working forwards, since no redundant information is restored.

It is worth noting that whatever method of dumping is used the recovery of the system affords a good opportunity to compact files into contiguous blocks. This reduces file access overheads at the expense of slightly lengthening the recovery procedure.

## 7.6 OPENING AND CLOSING FILES

We remarked in the last chapter that when an I/O stream is associated with a file the operating system must look up the device and location where the file is stored. This procedure is known as *opening* the file; the inverse procedure of *closing* the file is performed either explicitly when all I/O to the file has been completed or implicitly when the process using the file terminates.

To implement these operations we require within the operating system two procedures of the form

$$open\ (filename, mode) \qquad\qquad close\ (filename)$$

where *filename* is the name of the file to be opened or closed, and *mode* is the type of access required (for example read, write, or create). The operations performed by *open* are

(1)  Look up the directory entry for the file.
(2)  Check that the requesting process was instigated by a user with the requisite privileges for access in the specified mode.
(3)  Perform checks to ensure that if the file is already open for reading (possibly by another process) it cannot now be opened for writing, and

that if it is already open for writing it cannot now be opened at all. These checks will be described in a moment.

(4)   Ascertain the device and location where the file is stored. If the file is to be newly created then the location is specified by the space allocation routine.

(5)   Create a *file descriptor* which contains all information about the file relevant to forthcoming data transfers. The file descriptor, as mentioned in section 6.5, is used by I/O procedures as a source of information for constructing I/O requests, thus avoiding the necessity of going through the open procedure for each data transfer involving the file.

The information required in the file descriptor includes

(1)   the file name
(2)   the address of the device descriptor of the device on which the file is stored
(3)   the location of the first block in the file
(4)   the location of the next block to be read or written (assuming that access is sequential)
(5)   the mode of access

The file descriptor is pointed to from the appropriate stream descriptor of the process which has opened the file, as shown in figure 6.4a.

The read/write interlocks referred to in part (3) of the description of *open* may be implemented by including two extra items in the directory entry of each file. The first is a 'write bit' which is set whenever the file is opened for writing; the second is a 'use count' of the number of processes which currently have the file open for reading. A process may open a file for reading only if the write bit is zero, and may open it for writing only if the write bit and the use count are both zero. Unfortunately there is a problem with this technique in that several processes might simultaneously wish to open or close the same file, thus making simultaneous changes to the directory entry. This can be overcome by writing the *open* and *close* procedures as critical sections, each enclosed by the same mutual exclusion semaphore, but this has the serious disadvantage that if a process is interrupted while opening or closing a file then these operations are unavailable to all other processes.

An alternative technique is to form a list of the file descriptors of all files which are open on each particular device. This list can be pointed to from the device descriptor of the device concerned. When a file is to be opened the *open* procedure inspects the list to see whether any file descriptors already exist for the file, and if so what mode of access they indicate. The procedure refuses to open the file unless the read/write constraints are satisfied. A mutual exclusion semaphore can be used to protect the list from simultaneous access by processes which wish to open or close the same file at the same time. The disadvantage of this technique lies in the time required to inspect the list, which in a large multi-access system might easily contain 100 descriptors. This time is particularly critical since the list can be inspected by only one process at once, and if the process is interrupted then the list becomes inaccessible to other processes.

A partial solution to these problems is to divide each file descriptor into two separate structures: a *central file descriptor* for each open file and a *local file descriptor* for each process using a file. A local file descriptor is created each time a process opens a file, and all the local file descriptors for a particular file point to the single central file descriptor for that file. The central file descriptors are linked to the appropriate device descriptor (see figure 7.7). A central file descriptor contains information which is the same for any process using the file, namely

(1)    the file name
(2)    the address of the device descriptor of the device on which the file is stored
(3)    the location of the first block in the file
(4)    the use count for the file
(5)    the write bit for the file

A local file descriptor contains information which is particular to the process using the file, namely

(1)    the location of the next block to be read or written
(2)    the mode of access

plus a pointer to the central file descriptor for the file. The introduction of central file descriptors eliminates the storage of duplicate information in separate descriptors and reduces the length of the descriptor list for each device. It also reduces the amount of work the *open* and *close* procedures have to do in searching the descriptor list. More significantly, it allows mutual exclusion to be applied to each descriptor separately rather than to the list as a whole, and thus it avoids the bottleneck dangers mentioned earlier. The mutual exclusion semaphore can be held in the central file descriptor for each file.

A variation of this technique (Courtois *et al.*, 1971) is to replace the write bit in the central file descriptor by another semaphore $w$. The *open* and *close* procedures are then written to include the following pieces of code.

| *Open* | *Close* |
|---|---|
| **if** *mode* = read **then** | **if** *mode* = read **then** |
| **begin** *wait* (*mutex*); | **begin** *wait* (*mutex*); |
|     *usecount:* = *usecount* + 1; |     *usecount:* = *usecount* − 1; |
|     **if** *usecount* = 1 **then** *wait* (*w*); |     **if** *usecount* = 0 **then** *signal* (*w*); |
|     *signal* (*mutex*) |     *signal* (*mutex*) |
| **end** | **end** |
| **else** *wait* (*w*) | **else** *signal* (*w*) |

In this variation those access requests which are refused are implicitly queued on the semaphore $w$, while in the original version the system designer retains the freedom to queue requests or not, according to the application.

The operation of the *close* procedure is relatively simple. It consists of deleting the local file descriptor and decrementing the use count in the central file descriptor. If the use count is zero the central file descriptor is also deleted and the directory updated where necessary (if, for example, the file has just been created).

Deletion of a file may be treated as a call of *open* with an appropriate *mode* parameter. However this has the disadvantage that if the file is already open, as will often be the case with library files, the delete request will be refused. This

*Figure 7.7 Local and central file descriptors*

makes the replacement of library files somewhat awkward. A way round this problem is to include in each central file descriptor a 'delete pending bit' which is set whenever a delete request is made on an open file. The *close* procedure checks this bit: if it is set and the use count falls to zero the file can be deleted. Deletion is hastened if *open* refuses access to a file whose delete pending bit is set.

## 7.7 CONCLUSION

In this chapter we have discussed various aspects of filing systems for job-shop applications. The next step in the construction of our paper operating system is the adoption of a particular system based on the techniques we have described. This will give us another layer of our 'onion', consisting of code for implementing particular security and integrity mechanisms, for administering free space, and for opening and closing files. The additional permanent data structures are the file directories and whatever structure is used to record space allocation. Temporary data structures which exist only while a file is open are the local and central file descriptors. The current state of the system is shown in figure 7.8.

*Figure 7.8 Current state of the paper operating system*

# 8 *Resource Allocation and Scheduling*

Up to this point in the development of our paper operating system we have assumed that all processes have the resources they need. It is now time to consider how processes acquire their resources, and how a limited set of resources can be effectively shared among several processes. Our discussion of resource allocation will also include scheduling since the two functions are closely related: decisions on process priority can be dependent on where resources are committed, and the introduction of new processes into the system is clearly influenced by the amount of spare resource capacity. In fact scheduling, being concerned with the allocation of central processors, can be regarded as a subtopic of resource allocation as a whole.

## 8.1 GENERAL OBSERVATIONS

In an environment in which resources were unlimited a 'grab it when you need it' method of acquisition would be perfectly acceptable. Unfortunately it is rarely feasible to provide resources to satisfy the concurrent demands of all processes in the system, and so techniques must be devised to share a limited set of resources among a number of competing processes. The objectives of these techniques are to

(1) mutually exclude processes from unshareable resources
(2) prevent deadlock (see section 3.2) arising in respect of resource requests
(3) ensure a high level of resource utilisation
(4) allow all processes an opportunity of acquiring the resources they need within a 'reasonable' time

The reader will see that these objectives are not necessarily mutually consistent. In particular, the user satisfaction implied by objective (4) can generally be gained only by compromising objective (3). This is because the higher the level of resource utilisation the longer will be the average wait before a resource request can be granted. The trade-off between user satisfaction and resource utilisation is one of the criteria by which resource allocation and scheduling policies can be evaluated. In a real-time system with a guaranteed response time one would expect the trade-off to be in favour of the user; in a batch system it might be in favour of high utilisation. This can create a difficult managerial problem in a system which attempts to provide both batch and multi-access service.

It is useful to discuss resource allocation under two headings: the *mechanisms* and the *policies*. By *mechanisms* we mean the nuts and bolts aspect of how allocation is made. This includes such things as data structures for describing the state of resources, techniques for ensuring the exclusive use of unshareable resources, and means for queueing resource requests which cannot be granted immediately. The *policies* govern the ways in which the mechanisms are applied. They are concerned with the wisdom of granting requests even when the appropriate resources are available. This involves the questions of deadlock and system balance: an unwise allocation may lead to a situation in which some processes cannot proceed or in which the system is overloaded with respect to one particular class of resource. It is at this latter point that resource allocation becomes linked with scheduling, since the likelihood of overload can be reduced by judicious scheduling decisions on process priority and on the introduction of new processes into the system. We shall discuss both mechanisms and policies in the following sections.

## 8.2 ALLOCATION MECHANISMS

From the observations above it should be apparent that any element of a computing system which is in limited supply and which has to be shared can be regarded as a resource. In fact resources generally fall into one of the categories mentioned below. We shall review the allocation mechanisms for each category, giving consideration to what part of the system makes the allocation, the data structures used to describe the resources, and the means by which processes are queued while awaiting allocation.

### (1) Central Processors

We have already discussed in chapter 4 how a central processor is allocated by the dispatcher to the first non-running process in the processor queue. The data describing a central processor can be held in a processor descriptor which is similar to the device descriptor used for data relating to a peripheral (see chapter 6). The processor descriptor might typically contain

(a)   the processor identification
(b)   the current status – whether in user or supervisor mode
(c)   a pointer to the process descriptor of the current process

The processor descriptors can be contained within the central table, or be pointed to from it.

In a configuration in which processors are dissimilar the processor descriptors can be extended to hold an indication of the individual processor characteristics (whether it has floating point hardware for example). In this case each processor might be best suited to running a particular kind of process, and so might have its own processor queue pointed to from its descriptor. The processor queues are then analogous to the device request queues for peripherals. The assignment of processes to different processor queues is a subject still largely unexplored, and we shall not deal further with it here.

## (2) Memory

In chapter 5 we saw how memory can be allocated by the memory management layer of the operating system in both the paged and non-paged cases. The data structures describing the state of memory are the page tables, segment tables, or free block lists, depending on the machine architecture involved. A process waiting for the transfer of a new page or segment from secondary memory is made unrunnable, with the status bits in its process descriptor indicating the reason. Page and segment requests are queued as I/O request blocks by the memory management system, and serviced by the device handler for the appropriate secondary memory device.

## (3) Peripherals

We described in chapter 6 how in systems with stream based I/O an unshareable peripheral is allocated to a process when the corresponding stream is opened. In systems which do not use streams a peripheral may be allocated after a direct request to the operating system. In both cases the allocation mechanism is the same. The data structure describing a peripheral is its device descriptor, and processes awaiting allocation of a peripheral can be queued on a semaphore which is included in the descriptor. Mutual exclusion in the use of the peripheral is ensured by initialising the semaphore value to 1.

## (4) Backing Store

Backing store which is used in the implementation of virtual memory is allocated by the memory management system, and that used as file space is allocated by the filing system. Some operating systems, notably MULTICS, make no distinction between files and segments, so that the file store becomes part of the virtual memory and the filing system is responsible for all allocations. The data structure used for allocation is some kind of free block list or bit map as described in section 7.4.

Requests for file space are refused only when an individual user has exceeded his quota, or when all backing store is full. In neither case is it sensible to queue requests; the former situation can be resolved only by the user's own action, and the latter situation cannot be guaranteed to change within any small space of time.

**(5) Files**

An individual file may be regarded as a resource in the sense that several processes may wish to share it. As long as all processes operate in a 'read only' mode the resource is shareable; if one process wishes to write to the file then the resource is unshareable.

Allocation of a file to a process is made by the filing system when the file is opened, and write interlocks are achieved by the methods described in section 7.6. The data structures describing files are of course the file directories.

Job-shop filing systems do not usually queue file requests since simultaneous (non-read) requests are usually indicative of user error. However, in transaction processing or process control it may well be sensible to establish access queues within the filing system. These queues may be associated with semaphores as discussed in section 7.6.

It is apparent from the above review that allocation mechanisms are implemented at various levels of the operating system, each mechanism being found at the level appropriate to the resource being allocated. We shall see, however, that the policies for using the mechanisms must be global to the entire system.

**8.3 DEADLOCK**

The first resource allocation policies we consider are concerned with the problem of deadlock, which was described in section 3.2.

If resources are allocated to processes solely on the basis of their availability then deadlock may easily occur. In its simplest form deadlock will happen in the following circumstances: process $A$ is granted resource $X$ and then requests resource $Y$; process $B$ is granted resource $Y$ and then requests resource $X$. If both resources are unshareable and neither process will release the resource it holds then deadlock ensues. In general the necessary and sufficient conditions for deadlock (Coffman *et al.*, 1971) are

(1)    the resources involved are unshareable
(2)    processes hold the resources they have already been allocated while waiting for new ones
(3)    **resources cannot be pre-empted while being used**
(4)    a circular chain of processes exists such that each process holds resources which are currently being requested by the next process in the chain

The problem of deadlock may be solved by adopting one of the following strategies

(1)    prevent deadlock by ensuring at all times that at least one of the four conditions above does not hold
(2)    detect deadlock when it occurs and then try to recover
(3)    avoid deadlock by suitable anticipatory action

We consider each of these strategies in turn.

### (1) Deadlock Prevention

To prevent deadlock at least one of the four necessary conditions above must be denied.

Condition (1) is difficult to deny since some resources (for example a card reader or a writeable file) are by nature unshareable. However, the use of spooling (see section 6.6) can remove the deadlock potential of unshareable peripherals.

Condition (2) can be denied by stipulating that processes request all their resources at once and that they cannot proceed until all the requests are granted. This has the disadvantage that resources which are used only for a short time are nevertheless allocated and therefore inaccessible for long periods. It is, however, easy to implement, and may prove more economical in the long run than some more complex algorithm.

Condition (3) is easily denied by imposing the rule that if a process is refused a resource request then it must release all resources it currently holds, and if necessary request them again together with the additional resources. Unfortunately this Draconian strategy can be rather inconvenient in practice, since pre-empting a line printer (say) would result in the interleaving of the output from several jobs. Furthermore, even if a resource is conveniently pre-emptible, the overhead of storing and restoring its state at the time of pre-emption can be quite high. In the case of a central processor, however, the overhead is relatively small (namely storing the volatile environment of the current process), and the processor can always be regarded as pre-emptible.

Denial of condition (4) can be effected by imposing an order on resource types so that if a process has been allocated resources of type $k$ then it may request only resources of types which follow $k$ in the order. This ensures that the circular wait condition can never arise. The disadvantage is the constraint imposed on the natural order of resource requests, though this can be mitigated by placing commonly used resources early in the order.

An interesting example of these three ways of preventing deadlock occurs in OS/360 (Havender, 1968). In this system jobs are divided into 'job steps', and there is a job step initiator which is responsible for getting the resources necessary for each job step. The concurrent initiation of several job steps for different jobs is achieved by having several copies of the job step initiator. Deadlock between the copies is prevented by ensuring that each initiator always acquires resources in the order files, memory, peripherals. Deadlock between different job steps wishing to access the same files is prevented by making the initiator acquire files for a whole job at once. It should be noted that in this case pre-emption would not be appropriate, since a job would not want its files to be tampered with by alien job steps while it was itself between job steps. Neither can any reasonable order be placed on file requests. Deadlock over peripheral allocation is prevented by forcing jobs to release resources (except files) between job steps and to re-request them for the next step if required.

**(2) Deadlock Detection and Recovery**

If the prevention policies detailed above are considered too restrictive then an alternative approach may be acceptable. This allows the possibility of deadlock but relies on detecting it when it occurs and on being able to stage a recovery. The value of this approach depends on the frequency with which deadlock occurs and on the kind of recovery it is possible to make.

Detection algorithms work by detecting the circular wait expressed by condition (4) above. The state of the system at any time can be represented by a *state graph* in which the nodes are resources and an arc between nodes $A$ and $B$ implies that there exists a process which holds resource $A$ and is requesting resource $B$ (see figure 8.1).

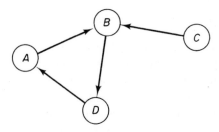

*Figure 8.1 Example state graph (resources A, B and D
are involved in deadlock)*

The circular wait condition is represented as a closed loop in the state graph (for example $A, B, D$ in figure 8.1). The detection algorithm maintains a representation of the state graph in some convenient form and inspects it at intervals for the existence of closed loops. The inspection may occur after each allocation or, since the overhead of doing this is probably too high, at fixed intervals of time.

Detection of deadlock is useful only if an acceptable attempt at recovery can be made. The definition of 'acceptable' can be stretched according to circumstance to include any of the following techniques, which are listed in order of increasing sophistication.

(a)    Abort all deadlocked processes. This is roughly equivalent to the Post Office burning the occasional sack of mail whenever it gets overloaded, but is the method adopted in most job-shop systems.

(b)    Restart the deadlocked processes from some intermediate checkpoint, if one exists. If naïvely applied this method may lead straight back to the original deadlock, but the nondeterminacy of the system will usually ensure that this does not happen.

(c)    Successively abort deadlocked processes until deadlock no longer exists. The order of abortion can be such as to minimise the cost of losing the investment of resources already used. This approach implies that after each abortion the detection algorithm must be reinvoked to see whether deadlock still exists.

(d)     Successively pre-empt resources from deadlocked processes until deadlock no longer exists. As in (c) the order of pre-emption can be such as to minimise some cost function. Reinvocation of the detection algorithm is required after each pre-emption. A process which has a resource pre-empted from it must make a subsequent request for the resource to be reallocated to it.

It is worth remarking before we leave the subject that detection of deadlock is often left to the computer operators rather than performed by the system itself. An observant operator will eventually notice that certain processes appear to be stuck, and on further investigation he will realise that deadlock has occurred. The customary recovery action is to abort and restart (if possible) the deadlocked processes.

## (3) Deadlock Avoidance

By deadlock avoidance we mean the use of an algorithm which will anticipate that deadlock is likely to occur and which will therefore refuse a resource request which would otherwise have been granted. This is a notion distinct from prevention, which ensures *a priori* that deadlock cannot occur by denying one of the necessary conditions.

A tempting line of approach to devising an avoidance algorithm is as follows. Before granting a resource request, tentatively change the state graph to what it would be if the request were granted, and then apply a deadlock detection algorithm. If the detection algorithm gives the all clear then grant the request; otherwise refuse the request and restore the state graph to its original form. Unfortunately this technique will not always work since it relies on the premise that if an allocation is going to result in deadlock then it will do so immediately. That this premise is false can be shown by study of figure 8.2 (due to Dijkstra), which illustrates a two-process, two-resource system.

The joint progress of processes $P_1$ and $P_2$ is represented by plotting a trajectory, shown in the diagram as the heavy arrowed line. The horizontal portions of the trajectory represent periods when $P_1$ is running, the vertical portions represent the periods when $P_2$ is running, and the sloping portions represent periods when both $P_1$ and $P_2$ are running simultaneously. (In a single processor configuration only horizontal and vertical portions can exist.) The trajectory is constrained from entering the shaded region on the diagram since this is an interval during which at least one of the resources $R_1$ and $R_2$ is required by both processes. The important point is that if the trajectory enters the region D then eventual deadlock is inevitable, since in that case there is no way that the trajectory can avoid meeting the shaded area (the trajectory can move only upwards and to the right, in the directions of positive progress). However, deadlock does not exist in region D itself, and so entering D would provoke no objection from any deadlock detection algorithm. Thus the use of a detection algorithm would not avoid deadlock in this case. To put it another way, a detection algorithm can see only one step ahead, whereas deadlock may be inevitable several steps ahead.

. It is apparent from the above discussion that a successful avoidance algorithm must possess some prior knowledge of the possible pattern of future events so that it can spot potential deadlocks before they arise. The type of prior know-ledge assumed is the feature which distinguishes one algorthm from another. We discuss below the *banker's algorithm*, which is probably the best known.

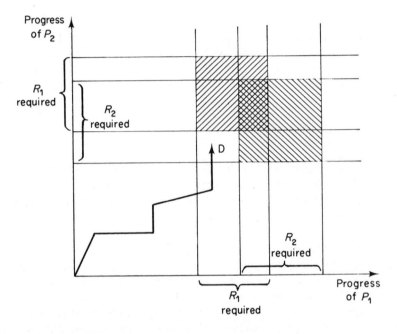

☐ interval during which $R_1$ is required by both processes

☐ interval during which $R_2$ is required by both processes

*Figure 8.2 Illustration of deadlock*

The prior knowledge demanded by the banker's algorithm is the maximum quantity of each resource which a process will require during its lifetime. We call this quantity the *claim* of a process on a resource. In batch systems this demand is quite reasonable, since job descriptions can be used to specify maximum resource requirements in advance. The algorithm allows a resource request only if

(a)  the request plus the current usage is less than the claim

and (b)  after doing so there exists a sequence in which all processes can run to completion even if they all demand their full claims.

Thus before making an allocation the algorithm checks that enough resources will be left to enable such a sequence to be constructed. It has been shown (Habermann, 1969) that the work involved in making the check is proportional to the square of the number of processes in the system.

As an example of how the algorithm works, consider again figure 8.2. The claims of $P_1$ and $P_2$ are each $R_1$ and $R_2$. Before entry into region D, $R_1$ is allocated to $P_1$ and $R_2$ is free. Thus there are sufficient resources left to run both $P_1$ and $P_2$ to completion even if both processes demand their full claims. The appropriate sequence in this case is $P_1$ followed by $P_2$. Inside region D, $R_1$ is allocated to $P_1$ and $R_2$ to $P_2$. Thus if both processes demand their claims there is no sequence (neither $P_1$ before $P_2$ nor vice versa) in which they can run to completion. The banker's algorithm therefore refuses entry into region D by denying the request for $R_2$ by $P_2$. $P_2$ will be suspended, and only $P_1$ will be able to run. The trajectory will therefore follow a horizontal course along the lower edge of the shaded area until $P_1$ releases $R_2$. At this point the original request by $P_2$ for $R_2$ can be granted since there are now sufficient resources available to complete both processes.

It should be noted that the banker's algorithm always allows for the worst possible case (that in which all processes demand their full claims). It may therefore sometimes refuse a request because deadlock *might* ensue, whereas if the request had been granted no deadlock would in fact have occurred. For example, in figure 8.2 entry into region D is forbidden because of the possibility that $P_1$ might exercise its claim on $R_2$ and $P_2$ might exercise its claim on $R_1$. If in fact either process chooses not to exercise its claim at an awkward moment then region D would be quite safe (since the shaded areas would not occupy the positions shown), and the refusal of $P_2$'s request for $R_2$ would have been unnecessarily restrictive. The tendency of the banker's algorithm towards over-cautiousness, together with the overheads of applying it, are the main drawbacks to its use.

We conclude our discussion of deadlock by considering the level in the operating system at which policies to deal with it should be implemented.

If a prevention strategy is used then all parts of the system which allocate resources operate under one or more of the constraints described earlier. The constraints can be implemented as part of the resource allocation mechanisms at the appropriate levels.

If detection is used then no alteration to the allocation mechanisms is required. The detection algorithm, which must have access to all allocation data structures, can be implemented at a high level, possibly within the scheduler itself. (The scheduler is described in later sections.)

In the case of deadlock avoidance all resource requests must be vetted by the avoidance algorithm. We shall see in the next section that all resource requests can be made via the scheduler, which thus becomes the natural place in which to implement the algorithm.

## 8.4 THE SCHEDULER

The term scheduling is generally understood to cover the questions of when to introduce new processes into the system and the order in which processes should run. As mentioned earlier these subjects are intimately related to resource allocation. In fact decisions on scheduling and decisions on resource allocation are so closely linked that it is often sensible to place responsibility for both in the hands of a single system process. We shall call this process the *scheduler*. The duties of the scheduler are described below.

### (1) Introduction of New Processes

In a batch system jobs awaiting execution are stored in a *job pool* which is held in secondary memory. (How they get there will be discussed in chapter 11.) The scheduler starts execution of a job by initiating an appropriate process such as compilation. The choice of which job to start next depends on the resources each job requires (as stated in its job description) and on the current pattern of resource allocation in the system. In order to achieve high throughput the scheduler should initiate a new process as soon as resource capacity warrants it.

In a multi-access system processes are created when users log-in to the system. Each new user increases the demand on resources, and access can be refused when the number of logged-in users is such as to increase response time to the limit of acceptability.

### (2) Assignment of Process Priorities

The order in which processes are run is determined either by the order of the processor queue or by the order in which the dispatcher selects processes from the queue. We suggested in chapter 4 that to minimise dispatching overheads the dispatcher should always pick the first eligible process in the queue; this implies that the order of the queue will be the determining factor. The scheduler is responsible for assigning priorities to processes so that when they become runnable they are linked into the appropriate place in the queue. Algorithms for determining suitable priorities will be discussed in the next section.

### (3) Implementation of Resource Allocation Policies

The policies implied here are those concerned with deadlock avoidance and with system balance; that is, with ensuring that no type of resource is either over- or under-committed. Criteria for evaluating balance will be discussed in the next section.

Since the behaviour of the system is largely determined by the activities of the scheduler it is important that the scheduler should have a high priority relative to other processes. If the scheduler has top priority the dispatcher will pick it whenever it is runnable in preference to all other processes. This ensures that the system reacts quickly to changes in circumstance, particularly to changes in demand. The occasions on which the scheduler might be activated are

(1)    a resource is requested
(2)    a resource is released
(3)    a process terminates
(4)    a new job arrives in the job pool (or a new user attempts to log-in)

It is instructive to note the analogy between interrupts and the scheduling events above. Both occur at unpredictable intervals, and both may cause the system to modify its behaviour. In the case of scheduling events the modifications are at a high level, affecting such global parameters as process priorities and the number of processes in the system; modifications due to interrupts are at a low level, affecting the runnability of processes and the allocation of the central processors. Interrupts may be expected to occur every few milliseconds, whereas scheduling events will probably occur only every second or so.

When the scheduler has finished its work it suspends itself by executing a *wait* operation on a semaphore; this semaphore is signalled whenever a scheduling event occurs. However, in an operating system which neither prevents nor avoids deadlock it is possible that no scheduling event does in fact occur. In this situation it is vital that the scheduler is reawakened in order to detect that deadlock prevails; this can be done by signalling the semaphore on certain clock interrupts, say every ten seconds.

The request and release of resources (the first two scheduling events above) can be implemented by providing two operating system procedures

*request resource (resource, result)*          *release resource (resource)*

These procedures place the necessary information about the resource concerned and the identity of the calling process in a data area accessible to the scheduler, and then signal the scheduler semaphore. The scheduler will respond according to criteria to be discussed in the next section. The second parameter of *request resource* is used to convey the result of the request, and may also give an indication of the reason for any refusal. Note that a request which is at first refused may be queued by the scheduler until the resource becomes available. In this case the request will eventually be granted and the *result* parameter of *request resource* will indicate this. The queueing operation and the associated delay are transparent to the requesting process.

A disadvantage of combining the scheduling and resource allocation functions in a single process is the overhead of process switching incurred whenever a resource is requested or released. If this overhead is thought to outweigh the gains that can be obtained from system balance and high resource utilisation then the two functions may be separated. In this case the routines *request resource* and *release resource* perform the resource allocation functions without invoking the scheduler.

## 8.5 SCHEDULING ALGORITHMS

The general objective of a scheduling algorithm is to arrange the pattern of work performed by the computing system so as to maximise some measure of user satisfaction. This measure may differ from system to system: in a batch environment it may be total throughput or the average turnround time for a certain class of job; in a multi-access system it may be the average response time offered to users, or the response time offered to certain kinds of interaction. The scheduling algorithm used will naturally depend on the goal desired.

We start by considering algorithms which are based on the assumption that central processors are the resources of prime importance. We have already implied at the start of this chapter that in many cases this assumption is false and that other resources may also be of importance. However, by studying processor-bound systems we may gain insight into the more complex cases to be discussed later.

*Figure 8.3 Scheduling model of a processor-bound system*

A general model of a processor-bound system is illustrated in figure 8.3. New processes arrive on the processor queue and are serviced by a number of processors. (We are assuming that the processors are identical.) After receiving a certain amount of service a process may be completed, in which case it leaves the system; otherwise it is returned to the queue to await further service at a later time. The model represents processes only in the runnable and running states; the omission of the blocked state of chapter 4 reflects the fact that in a processor-bound system the only significant delays which can occur are due to waiting in the processor queue. A particular scheduling algorithm is characterised by the order of processes in the queue and the conditions under which processes are fed back into it. We consider several popular algorithms below.

### (1) Shortest Job First

As the name implies the queue is ordered according to the running time required by each process. The algorithm is suitable only for batch systems, where an estimate of the running time can be acquired from the job description. Its aim is to minimise the turnround time of short jobs, and it is therefore best used in an environment in which short jobs form the bulk of the load. In its simplest form the algorithm allows all processes to run to completion, but a modification can be made by which a new process may pre-empt a processor if it has a running time less than that required to finish the current process. This version, known as *pre-emptive shortest job first*, is even more favourable to short jobs. Another modification, which ensures that long jobs are not delayed indefinitely, is gradually to increase the priority of a process according to the length of time it has been in the queue.

## (2) Round Robin

This algorithm was developed as a means of giving rapid response to short service requests when running times are not known in advance. Each process in the system receives a fixed quantum of service before being returned to the end of the queue. The queue is therefore circular, and ordered by length of time since the last service. Processes which require lengthy service will cycle round the queue several times before being completed, while processes whose service time is less than the quantum will terminate on the first cycle. The round robin algorithm was used in the early time-sharing system CTSS (Corbató *et al.*, 1962) and has subsequently been implemented with several variations in many other systems. Most variations have the aim of reducing the tendency of the system to collapse under heavy loading. Analysis and experience both show that if the load becomes too heavy for a given quantum size then performance is suddenly degraded. One way of overcoming this is to increase the quantum size as the number of processes rises. This increases the probability that a process will terminate within the quantum, and so reduces the overhead of process switching.

## (3) Two-level Queue

This is another variation of the round robin algorithm which attempts to overcome sudden load degradation. Processes which are not completed within a fixed number of quanta are syphoned off into a 'background' queue which is serviced only if there are no other processes in the system. The background queue may itself be treated on a round robin basis with a larger quantum, or it may be simply first come, first served. The two-level system is often used in mixed batch and multi-access environments, where the longer batch processes tend to sink into the background and are serviced only when no terminal initiated processes are present. The algorithm can of course be generalised to a *multi-level system* if this is considered appropriate. An example of this occurs in the DEC System-10 Monitor, where there are three round robin queues with quanta set at 0.02 seconds, 0.25 seconds, and 2 seconds respectively. (These values may in fact be changed if desired.)

The optimal values of the parameters of the round robin algorithm and its descendants, such as quantum size and when to move processes to a background queue, are difficult to determine analytically (but see Coffman and Denning, 1973, for some attempts). Approximations may be found by simulation, and adjusted after experience of real life running conditions.

The algorithms above form the basis of most popular scheduling policies. Other algorithms and variations can be found in the excellent survey by Coffman and Kleinrock (1968). One particular variation of note is to allow the inclusion of externally specified priorities. The effect is that processes with high external priority receive a better service than would be the case with the pure form of an algorithm. This enables users with tight deadlines or VIP status to obtain better response from the system, though they may be charged more for the privilege.

Systems in which central processors are not the sole resources of importance can be described by the model shown in figure 8.4. This model differs from that of figure 8.3 by the inclusion of the blocked state, in which processes wait for resource requests or I/O transfers. The addition of this state greatly increases the complexity of the model. Firstly, the state is characterised not by a single queue but by a multiplicity of queues associated with the various semaphores which cause blocking to occur. Secondly, processes move from the blocked to the runnable state after events such as the signalling of a semaphore which occur at unpredictable intervals. The movement of processes between queues can be studied for different scheduling strategies either by formal analysis or by simulation (Coffman and Denning, 1973; Svobodova, 1976), though the complexity of the model makes both techniques difficult to apply.

*Figure 8.4 General scheduling model*

The reader will see from figure 8.4 that one of the aims of a scheduling algorithm could be to minimise the number of transitions from the running to the blocked state. Since the transitions due to I/O transfers are outside its control it follows that the algorithm should minimise the number of resource requests which are refused. This implies that processes should be introduced into the system only if their likely resource demands can be satisfied by the resources currently available. This policy is more easily implemented in batch systems, where maximum resource demands can be specified in advance, than in multi-access systems, where demands are virtually unpredictable. An example of batch implementation was the Atlas operating system, in which jobs were divided into three classes: short jobs, requiring little processor time and no esoteric peripherals; magnetic tape jobs, whose name is self-explanatory, and long jobs, comprising the rest. The scheduler attempted to maintain at least one job of each class in the system at any given time.

It is worth noting that policies such as this will not necessarily result in high resource utilisation. The reason is that a process is unlikely to use throughout its life all the resources of which it has given notice. The resources claimed, and allowed for by the scheduler, may therefore lie idle for considerable periods. If higher utilisation is required the scheduler must make policy decisions on resource allocation not only when introducing a new process but also when each resource request or release occurs. The criteria for making such decisions and for assigning process priorities are generally empirical; we discuss a few of them below.

(1)    Processes which possess a large number of resources may be given high priority in an attempt to speed their completion and regain the resources for deployment elsewhere. The danger of pursuing this strategy is that large jobs might monopolise the machine or that users may generate dummy resource requests in order to gain favourable treatment. This latter danger can be avoided in a batch system by ensuring that jobs with small resource requirements are selected for running in preference to others.

(2)    Processes which possess a large number of resources could have further requests granted whenever possible. The justification is similar to that above, and again there is a danger that large jobs might monopolise the system.

(3)    Memory allocation in paged machines can be performed according to the working set principle described in chapter 5.

(4)    Operating system processes should have priorities which reflect the urgency of the functions they perform. The scale will range from the scheduler itself at the top to such processes as the incremental file dumper at the bottom. Most system processes will have higher priorities than user processes.

(5)    As a special case of (4) peripheral device handlers should have high priority. In general the faster the device the higher should be the priority of the associated handler. This ensures that peripherals are kept busy as much as possible, thereby reducing the potential of I/O bottlenecks. If spooling is used then the spoolers should also have high priority.

(6)    Unless deadlock prevention measures are in force all resource requests should be subjected to a deadlock avoidance algorithm.

(7)    The overhead in making scheduling decisions should not be out of proportion to the ensuing gains.

The considerations above may be used to modify one of the processor scheduling algorithms described earlier. The result will be an algorithm in which process priorities are continually being updated according to the pattern of resource demand and the state of the system. The performance of such an algorithm is difficult to gauge except by observation; it can often be substantially improved by quite minor alterations to its parameters. An interesting example of such an improvement arose in the DEC System-10 Monitor. In an early version of the scheduling algorithm processes which re-entered the runnable state after being blocked while awaiting teletype I/O were placed on the end of the first level processor queue. This procedure was subsequently changed so as to place these processes on the front of the first level queue. The improvement of response to multi-access users was dramatic.

We may summarise this section by saying that the number of possible scheduling algorithms is very large, but that at present we have no means of selecting an optimal algorithm for a specific case other than by experiment. Analysis and simulation can be of some help, but their value is restricted by the complexity of most systems.

## 8.6 PROCESS HIERARCHIES

We saw in section 8.4 that the scheduler is responsible for initiating new processes. Thus in a sense the scheduler is the parent of all processes introduced into the system. Moreover, it is responsible for the welfare of its offspring in that it governs policies of resource allocation and influences the order in which processes are selected by the dispatcher. This parental role need not be restricted to the scheduler; it can be extended to other processes by allowing them the capability to

(1)    create subprocesses
(2)    allocate to their subprocesses a subset of their own resources (the resources being returned when the subprocess terminates)
(3)    determine the relative priority of their subprocesses

The effect is to enable the creation of a hierarchy of processes with the scheduler at the head. Thus the natural form of the process structure is no longer the simple list of chapter 4, but a tree as shown in figure 8.5. The tree is partially threaded by the processor queue, which links all the nodes (processes) which are currently runnable.

The advantages of a hierarchical organisation are twofold. First, it allows a process which performs several independent tasks to create a subsidiary process for each task so that the tasks may be executed in parallel. Of course nothing is gained on a machine with a single central processor since only apparent concurrency can be achieved, but when several processors are available real gains may result.

Second, it allows several versions of the operating system, each oriented towards a different application, to run independently and in parallel. The different versions, or subsystems, will each be based on the facilities provided by the system nucleus (see chapter 4,) but may use different algorithms for the implementation of the higher system functions which appear in the outer layers. Thus each subsystem is a particular version of our 'onion', though all subsystems have the same core. The various subsystems each implement a virtual machine which is suitable for a particular class of users, and all the virtual machines coexist in the same physical configuration.

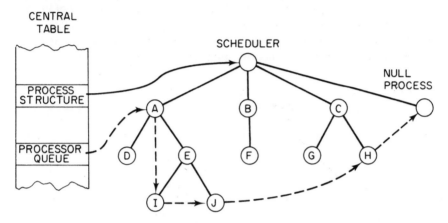

*Figure 8.5 A process hierarchy*

As an example consider figure 8.6, which illustrates a situation in which two different subsystems are responsible for batch and on-line work respectively. The performance of the two subsystems is governed by the resources and relative priorities allocated by the scheduler; within these constraints each subsystem can control its subordinate processes according to any appropriate algorithms. Within the batch subsystem, for example, all I/O may be spooled and user processes ordered on a shortest first principle; within the on-line subsystem I/O may be unspooled and processes ordered in a round robin. One can imagine an extension of the hierarchy in which, for instance, the batch subsystem is divided into further subsystems which handle different classes of job.

One advantage of the subsystem arrangement is the coexistence of different virtual machines. Another is the ability to develop new versions of an operating system while the old version runs in parallel. Against this must be set the loss of global control over resource allocation which results from the way in which resources are passed up and down the process structure. Resources which have been allocated to a subsystem or to an inferior process, and which are not being used, cannot be transferred elsewhere in the system unless they are first returned to a common ancestor. Since processes are free to allocate subsets of their resources as they wish there is no guarantee that the overall pattern of resource utilisation will in any way be optimal.

The assignment of priorities by a process to its offspring can also create problems. Unless some restrictions are imposed it is possible for a process to gain an unfair scheduling advantage by delegating its task to a subprocess to which it assigns a very high priority. One form of restriction which will overcome this problem is to insist that all priorities are assigned relative to that of the parent process, and that the range over which relative priorities may vary successively decreases at each level down the hierarchy. For example, suppose that in figure 8.5 the range of relative priorities at the top level is 0–99, and at the second level is 0–9, and so on. Then if the priority of process B is 20 no subprocess of B may have a priority outside the range 20±9. This implies that if the priority of process A is greater than 29 then B cannot gain any advantage over A by splitting itself up into subprocesses. If the priority of A is greater than 39 then all subprocesses of A will be guaranteed preference over subprocesses of B.

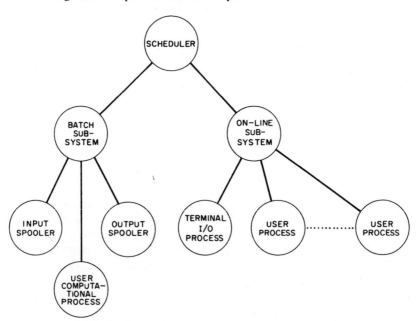

*Figure 8.6 Example of multiple subsystems*

In the situation shown in figure 8.6 the relative priorities assigned by the scheduler to the batch and on-line subsystems effectively determine the response of the system to the two classes of job. A large difference in priority between the subsystems will ensure that one class of user always gains preference over the other, a small difference will result in competition for the central processor(s) on more equal terms. The relative priority of processes within each subsystem is, as mentioned earlier, a matter for the subsystem concerned.

One operating system which displays a hierarchical process structure is that on the RC–4000 computer (Hansen, 1970). The nucleus of this system is referred to as the Monitor, and the head of the hierarchy, which corresponds to our scheduler, is called the Basic Operating System. Up to 23 processes (the restriction is for reasons of space) may exist in the structure, and resources are passed from parents to offspring as described above. One difference between the RC-4000 system and the one we have outlined is that parents cannot assign priorities to their children; all processes have equal priority except in so far as they are selected by the dispatcher on a round robin basis.

A limited hierarchy is also implemented by the IBM VM/370 operating system (VM stands for Virtual Machine). The structure is restricted to three levels: at the root is the VM/370 system itself, at the next level may occur any of a number of other standard IBM operating systems (acting as subsystems), and at the lowest level are the user tasks. The standard operating systems which run at the second level provide various virtual machines on the same configuration. The dispatcher works according to a two-level round robin discipline which can be modified by assigning relative priorities to each subsystem.

The implementation of a hierarchical process structure requires the provision of the system procedures

> *create process (name, relative priority)*    *delete process (name)*
> *start process (name)*                          *stop process (name)*

The function of *create process* is to set up a process descriptor for the new process and link it into the process structure. *Start process* adds the process descriptor to the processor queue, that is it marks the process as eligible to run. *Stop process* and *delete process* perform the inverse functions, and allow a parent to control its children. Children may of course terminate of their own accord, in which case the use of *stop process* is unnecessary. All four procedures manipulate process descriptors or the processor queue, and should therefore be implemented within the system nucleus. The procedures *request resource* and *release resource* described in section 8.4 are amended so as to invoke the parent process rather than the scheduler. The parent process is thus made responsible for allocation to its offspring.

## 8.7 CONTROL AND ACCOUNTING

The previous sections have been concerned with the allocation of resources on a time scale which is comparable with job running times. We now turn our attention to longer term aspects of resource allocation, that is to such questions as charging for resource usage, estimating and influencing the pattern of demand, and ensuring that all users receive an appropriate proportion of the computing facilities available. These matters are usually described by the term *resource control*. Strictly speaking, resource control is the concern of the computer manager rather than the operating system designer, but unless the designer provides the appropriate tools the manager is impotent. In particular the designer must provide tools for measurement, since without measurement no control is possible.

The aims of resource control depend on the installation concerned. Broadly speaking installations are of two types; *service* and *in-house*. The purpose of a service installation, such as exists in a bureau, is to provide computing facilities for a number of paying users. No restrictions, other than the ability to pay, are placed upon users; indeed it is in the interests of management to sell as many facilities to as many users as possible. Resource control is thus reduced to *accounting*, that is, to recording the amount of each chargeable resource used and billing each user accordingly.

An in-house installation on the other hand is owned by a single company, university, or other institution, and provides facilities only to members of that institution. Because of constraints imposed on his budget the manager has the problem of dealing with a demand for service which nearly always exceeds the installation's capacity. Unlike a bureau no profit is gained from providing service, and so the option of increasing capacity to meet demand is not usually open. Thus the manager must ration the resources available according to the relative needs or importance of the various users. Resource control in this case provides a tool for discrimination between users. It must fulfil the dual function of accounting for resources and ensuring that no user exceeds his ration.

It should be clear that the control mechanisms required for service installations are a subset of those required for in-house installations. We shall therefore concentrate on the latter.

### (1) Restriction of Access

Access to facilities which entail heavy resource usage can be denied to certain classes of user such as junior programmers or students. Again, users working in multi-access mode might be restricted to editing and small scale testing, while batch users are allowed free range of all facilities.

### (2) Rationing

A rationing policy may be either long or short term, or a combination of both. Short term rationing applies a limit to the amount of resource, such as processor time or memory space, which can be used by a single job. In long term rationing a budget is given to each user indicating the amount of resources which he can use in a given period, for example, a week or a month. Attempts by a user to exceed his ration result in job abortion or refusal of access to the system.

Both methods of control can be implemented by maintaining an accounting file which contains the following information for each accredited user of the system.

(1) The user identification. This is an 'account number' quoted by the user when he logs in or at the head of a job description. It serves to identify the user to the system.

(2)     A password known only to the user and to the system. This is presented by the user as proof of his identity. (Passwords are not normally required in batch systems, since their secrecy is difficult to maintain when punched on cards or paper tape.)

(3)     A 'permission vector' in which each bit represents the permission to use a certain facility. Permission is granted only if the appropriate bit is set.

(4)     The resource limits for a single job.

(5)     The budget for the current accounting period.

(6)     The resources still outstanding in the budget for the current period.

The details of how control is applied vary from system to system. In batch-oriented systems the outstanding resource balance is debited at the end of each job, and jobs are accepted by the scheduler only if the balance is positive. An alternative is to accept a job only if its stated resource requirements are less than the current balance; this prevents a user exceeding his ration by running a large job when his balance is almost zero. In a multi-access system the balance may be debited at regular intervals during a terminal session and the user forcibly logged off (after an appropriate warning) if the balance reaches zero.

Rationing may be applied to each resource separately or, more commonly, the usage of each resource may be compounded through some specified charging formula into some kind of global resource consumption units. In this case the relative weights given to each resource in the charging formula are chosen so as to reflect the resource's importance or scarcity value. An example of such a charging formula, taken from the Essex University DEC System-10 is

$$\text{number of units used} = (133.0P + 6.0C + 13.3K + 5.5W)$$

where

$$
\begin{aligned}
P &= \text{central processor time in seconds} \\
C &= \text{terminal connect time in seconds} \\
K &= \text{memory occupancy, that is the integral} \\
  &\quad\ \text{over processor time of the number of} \\
  &\quad\ \text{1024 word memory blocks used} \\
W &= \text{number of disc transfers}
\end{aligned}
$$

It is worth noting that the parameters in a charging formula can be altered in order to influence the way in which users work. For example, a dramatic increase in the charge for terminal connect time would encourage users to make greater use of batch facilities, while an increase in the memory occupancy charge might be an incentive to writing small jobs.

Another important feature of a rationing policy is that the total allocated amount of each resource should be related to the amount of the resource which the system can supply in the given time period. The amount allocated and the amount in supply need not be equal, since there is a good chance that most users will not consume their entire allocation; the degree of safe over-allocation can be gauged by experience. In the case of global charging formulae the allocation and supply are more difficult to match, for if all users decided to use their allocation in the form of the same resource then the system could not cope. In practice the existence of a large user population makes this eventuality unlikely.

More sophisticated rationing policies (for example, Hartley, 1970) may employ different charging rates at different times of the day. This encourages use of the machine at unpopular times and gives a more even distribution of the work load. Similarly, charges may vary according to the external priority a user has requested for his work.

The system designer's responsibility is to provide the tools for implementing policies such as just described. These tools include

(1)    routines for adminstering the accounting file
(2)    mechanisms for measuring resource usage
(3)    mechanisms for refusing facilities to users who have overdrawn their budgets

The measurement of resource usage is a function which is distributed throughout the system at the points where resources are allocated. It can be greatly facilitated by the provision of suitable hardware, such as a counter in the disc controller to record the number of transfers. A real-time clock is of course essential to accurate measurement. Measurements on an individual process can be stored as part of the process descriptor, and statistics on total system usage can be gathered in a central file. The latter figures can be regarded as an indicator of system performance and used as a basis of comparison and enhancement.

Consideration should perhaps also be given to the question of whether operating system overheads should be charged to the user. On the one hand it can be argued that the operating system is acting on behalf of the user, and that the user should therefore be charged. This would have the beneficial side effect of encouraging users to write programs in such a way as to minimise system overhead, by avoiding redundant file accesses for example. On the other hand the overheads will vary according to the current load, and it might be considered unfair to charge a user more simply because the machine is busy or because his job interacts unfavourably with some other job which happens to be present at the same time. It could also be argued that the ordinary user should not be expected to acquire the detailed knowledge of the operating system that would be needed for him to modify his work to reduce overheads. A possible compromise is to charge the user for all system activities, such as I/O handling, performed specifically on his behalf, but not to charge for activities such as process switching which are outside his control. However, even this leaves some areas subject to dispute; paging traffic for example is dependent both on the user, who can increase the locality of his memory references, and on the current pressure of demand for memory. Ultimately decisions in this field are necessarily arbitrary, and must be left to the individual designer.

## 8.8 SUMMARY

In this chapter we have seen how policies for resource allocation and scheduling can be implemented in a single process which we called the scheduler. We have described how the functions of the scheduler can be extended to other processes, thus establishing a hierarchical process structure. The nucleus of our paper operating system has been enlarged by the inclusion of procedures for creating and deleting processes. The mechanisms for allocating resources and for measuring resource usage are distributed thoughout the system at the levels appropriate to the resources concerned. The current state of our system is as shown in figure 8.7.

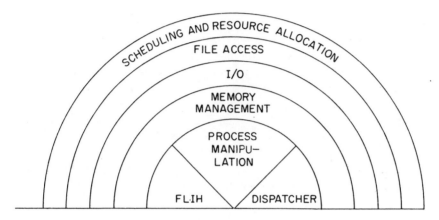

*Figure 8.7 Current state of the paper operating system*

The additional data structures are

(1)  a record of available resources
(2)  for each process a list of resources allocated to it, pointed to from the process descriptor
(3)  if deadlock detection is employed then a representation of the state graph
(4)  if deadlock avoidance is employed then a record of resource claims and allocations
(5)  a possible elaboration of the processor queue to include several levels
(6)  a possible modification of the process structure which turns it into a tree
(7)  an accounting file

# 9 *Protection*

We have already alluded several times to the fact that processes within a computing system must be protected from each other's activities. We have introduced mechanisms at various points in our paper operating system which ensure that the memory, files, and resources belonging to a process cannot be accessed by another process except in a controlled manner. The mechanisms have been **distributed** throughout the system in such places as the memory addressing hardware, file directories, and resource allocation procedures, and have functioned more or less independently of each other. In this chapter we take a closer look at the subject of protection as a whole and indicate how it is possible to implement protection mechanisms on a unified system-wide basis.

## 9.1 MOTIVATION

The motivation for protection mechanisms in a multi-user computing system may be summarised as follows.

### (1) Protection from Faults

When several processes, possibly working for different users, are executing on the same machine it is clearly desirable that faults in any one of them should not be allowed to affect the running of the others. Few users would tolerate a system in which every process had to be guaranteed fault-free before they could be confident that their own work would be run without interference. Mechanisms must therefore be devised to erect 'fire walls' between the different processes in the system. Protection from faults applies not only to user processes but also to the operating system itself. If the operating system can be corrupted by faults in a user process then it is unlikely to perform well (or at all) for very long.

Protection is desirable even in the case of a single user with a private machine. In this situation protection can be an aid to debugging by limiting the propagation of errors and localising the original source. Even when programs are fully debugged protection can minimise the damage caused by hardware malfunction or operator error. These considerations apply even more forcefully in multi-user systems.

## (2) Protection from Malice

At a time when computers are increasingly being used for storing and processing data bases, many of which contain confidential information, it is essential that the security of data can be guaranteed. The guarantee may be required for commercial reasons, as in the case of an installation which provides a service to users with divergent interests, or it may be required for reasons of privacy. For example, employees of government agencies such as the Health Service or the Inland Revenue must be prevented from accessing confidential personal records without authorisation. The safeguards required for data apply equally to programs. For example, a company which has invested a great deal of money in developing a program which it intends to sell or hire will not be happy if its customers or competitors are able to copy the program and install it elsewhere. Similarly, the Inland Revenue would be dismayed to find that one of its employees had modified a program so that he had paid no tax for the past five years.

An operating system itself is a collection of programs and data which must be protected from malice. It is not difficult to imagine a user modifying an unprotected system so that his jobs are always scheduled first, or so that he is never charged for the resources he uses.

If protection were simply a matter of isolating all processes from each other then adequate mechanisms could readily be devised. Unfortunately processes may well have legitimate grounds for wishing to share resources, access common data, or execute the same programs. A worthwhile protection system must therefore allow legitimate sharing while preventing unauthorised interference. It is the coexistence in a computing system of elements of both co-operation and competition which makes protection a problem.

## 9.2 DEVELOPMENT OF PROTECTION MECHANISMS

Protection in the elementary sense of totally excluding unauthorised users from the system can be achieved by requiring that a user presents some proof of his identity when he logs-in or submits a job. The user generally does this by quoting his account number, which is used in charging for the resources used, and a password known only to himself and the operating system. The account number and the password are checked against the system accounting file, as described in section 8.7. Provided the accounting file is inaccessible to users, and provided that each user keeps his password secret, then entry to the system can be made by authorised users only. Unfortunately this latter proviso is difficult to enforce in practice since users have a habit of disclosing their passwords, either inadvertently or through a misplaced sense of generosity. In batch systems in particular it is difficult to keep passwords secret since they have to be punched on cards or paper tape, and consequently many batch systems do not demand passwords at all. Even in multi-access systems where the users observe strict secrecy it has been proved that a determined intruder, through a process of inspired trial and error, can eventually discover a valid password and penetrate the system. We shall not discuss this topic any further here, but shall concentrate for the rest of this chapter on the protection measures that can be applied once users have gained some form of access (legitimate or otherwise) to the system.

A rudimentary form of protection can be achieved by including in the hardware of the host machine a *mode switch* and a pair of *base and limit registers*. The mode switch governs the ability to execute privileged instructions as described in section 4.1, and the base and limit registers demarcate the area of memory accessible to a process when in user mode (see section 5.3). Information which is resident in main memory is protected by the base and limit registers, whose values can be altered only when the processor is in supervisor mode; information on backing store is protected by virtue of the fact that I/O instructions are privileged and thus all data transfers can occur only via the operating system. Validation of the transfers can be achieved by using information held in the file directories when the files are opened and closed, as described in chapter 7.

This form of protection is found in most computers of the mid 1960s (for example the ICL 1900 series). It is unsatisfactory in that it is an 'all or nothing' solution to the protection problem: a process either has no privileges (executing in user mode) or all privileges (executing in supervisor mode). Thus, for example, processes executing any system procedures have the same absolute privileges, irrespective of whether they need them. Furthermore, sharing of data or programs between processes is possible only by making their memory spaces overlap, in which case the processes are completely unprotected from each other.

A more flexible protection scheme can be implemented if the host machine is equipped with segmentation hardware (see section 5.3). In this case the address space of each process is divided into logical segments, and each segment can be given a particular degree of protection (such as execute only or read only) by incorporating a protection indicator into its descriptor. The situation is illustrated in figure 5.5. The memory addressing hardware checks all accesses to the segment to ensure that the protection specified in the descriptor is not violated.

Since each process references its segments through its own set of segment descriptors (held in its segment table) it is possible for two processes to reference the same physical segment through descriptors which have different protection indicators. This allows segments to be shared between processes with different access rights. Figure 9.1 shows an example in which a process $A$ reads information which is deposited in a buffer by process $B$. The buffer appears as a segment in the address spaces of both $A$ and $B$; its descriptor in process $A$ specifies read only access, while its descriptor in process $B$ allows write access. Both descriptors point to the same location in memory.

Although this scheme is an improvement on the previous one it still does not provide us with adequate protection. The reason is that the access rights which a process has for a segment remain unchanged throughout the process's lifetime. This means that whatever program or procedure the process is executing it maintains constant privileges over all its segments. (An exception to this is when the process enters supervisor mode, when it assumes absolute privileges over all segments.) A preferable arrangement, not provided for by the scheme above, is that a process should at all times possess only those privileges which it needs for the activity it is currently engaged in. This philosophy of 'minimum necessary privilege' is essential to the aim of limiting the effects of erroneous or malicious processes.

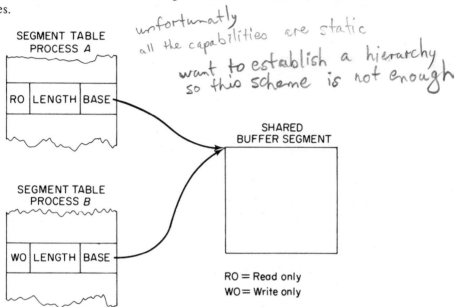

*unfortunatly all the capabilities are static*
*want to establish a hierarchy so this scheme is not enough*

*Figure 9.1 Segment sharing with different access privileges*

As an example consider again processes *A* and *B* of figure 9.1. If use of the buffer is extended to include two-way communication between the processes then both *A* and *B* require write access to it. This means that each process has the ability to write to the buffer even at those times when it is supposed to be reading, and thus the information in the buffer cannot be guaranteed against malfunction in either process. What is required is that the access privileges of *A* and *B* for the buffer should be dependent on whether they are currently engaged in sending or receiving information. Thus when either process is executing a procedure for sending information it should have write access to the buffer, but when it is executing a procedure for receiving information the access should be read only.

As a result of this discussion we introduce the idea of a *domain* of protection (other terms are *sphere*, *context* and *regime*) in which a process executes. Each domain defines a set of privileges or *capabilities* which can be exercised by a process executing in it. A change of capabilities can be achieved only by a transition from one domain to another; we naturally insist that such transitions are strictly controlled.

Primitive examples of domains are the supervisor and user modes of execution mentioned earlier. When a process executes in supervisor mode its capabilities include the right to execute privileged instructions and to reference the whole memory; when it is in user mode its capabilities are restricted to the use of non-privileged instructions and to accessing only its own memory space. For reasons discussed earlier this two-domain system is inadequate for our purposes: what we have in mind is a more complex arrangement in which a number of domains define a large variety of capabilities and in which a process runs in the domain which contains just those capabilities which allow it to transact its legitimate business. We shall examine in the following sections how such an arrangement can be implemented.

It is worth noting at this point that capabilities for all objects which require protection can be expressed in terms of capabilities for memory segments. Access to a system data structure can, for example, be expressed in terms of access to the segment containing it while permission to operate a peripheral device depends on access to the segment containing the device descriptor. (Some computers, such as the PDP-11 and most microprocessors, incorporate device addresses within the overall address space; in these computers access to devices can be controlled in exactly the same way as access to memory.) This observation leads to a significant simplification of protection schemes since it allows all protection to be performed by means of segment capabilities, which in turn can be implemented as part of the memory addressing mechanisms. This approach is followed in the schemes described below.

## 9.3 A HIERARCHICAL PROTECTION SYSTEM

In this section we describe the protection scheme implemented in MULTICS (Graham, 1968; Schroeder and Saltzer, 1972) which was one of the earliest systems to treat protection in a generalised way. The description is somewhat simplified, but will serve to illustrate the ideas behind a hierarchically organised protection scheme. Domains in MULTICS are called *rings*, and are ordered so that each ring contains a subset of the capabilities of the one inside it. Conceptually the arrangement can be viewed as shown in figure 9.2, where the progression from the outermost (high numbered) rings to the innermost (low numbered) rings bestows successively greater privileges. The reader will see that this is a refinement of the supervisor/user mode system of protection, which can in fact be considered as a two-ring system.

A ring in MULTICS is a collection of segments, and for the moment we shall consider that each segment is assigned to one and only one ring. Procedures which require a large number of privileges reside in segments in inner rings, while procedures needing less privileges, or which cannot be trusted to be error-free, are contained in segments in outer rings.

In order to identify the ring to which a segment belongs its segment descriptor is extended to include a field holding the ring number. The program counter is similarly extended to identify the ring in which the current process is executing (that is, the ring number of the segment from which it is executing instructions). The protection indicator in the segment descriptor includes flags which denote whether the segment can be written, read, or executed (see figure 9.3). A process executing in ring $i$ has no access whatever to segments in ring $j$, where $j < i$; its access to segments in ring $k$, where $k \geqslant i$, is governed by the access indicators of the segments concerned. In other words access to inner rings is prohibited, while access to outer rings is subject to the access indicators. An attempt by a process to cross a ring boundary by calling a procedure in a different ring results in the generation of an error trap. The trap causes entry to a special trap handler which performs certain checks on the transfer of control. These checks will be described in a moment.

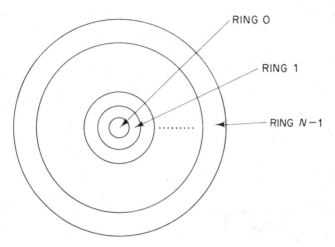

*Figure 9.2 Rings of protection*

ACCESS
INDICATOR

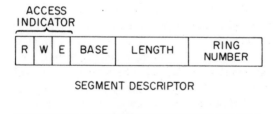

SEGMENT DESCRIPTOR

| RING
NUMBER | SEGMENT
NUMBER | WORD
NUMBER |
|---|---|---|

PROGRAM COUNTER

*Figure 9.3 MULTICS segment descriptor and program counter*

The mechanism described above is adequate for the provision of hierarchical protection. However, the fact that a segment is assigned to only one ring leads to inefficiencies arising from the large number of procedure calls across ring boundaries. A more flexible arrangement, adopted in MULTICS, is to allocate each segment to a set of consecutive rings known as its *access bracket*. The ring field of the segment descriptor then contains two integers $n1$ and $n2$ which specify the lowest and highest rings of the access bracket. A call by a process executing in ring $i$ to a procedure in a segment with access bracket $(n1,n2)$ does not now cause a trap so long as $n1 \leqslant i \leqslant n2$, and in this case control remains in ring $i$.

If $i > n2$ or $i < n1$ a trap is generated, and the corresponding trap handler must decide whether the call is to be allowed. (The trap handler may be a procedure in ring 0 or, as in MULTICS, it may be largely integrated into the memory addressing hardware.) The case $i < n1$ represents an outward call, that is, a transfer of control to a ring with lesser privileges, and can therefore always be allowed. However, the parameters of the call may refer to segments which are inaccessible to the called procedure because of its inferior status. In this case the parameters must be copied into a data area accessible to the called procedure.

A call in the reverse direction $(i > n2)$ is more difficult to handle. Since the call represents a transfer of control to a ring with higher privileges care must be taken that the caller cannot in any way cause the called procedure to malfunction. A first step in this direction is to allow calls only from rings which are not too far distant from the access bracket of the called procedure. An integer $n3$ $(n3 > n2)$ held in each segment descriptor is used to define the limit of the segment's *call bracket*; a call from ring $i$, where $i > n3$, is not permitted. Further, each segment possesses a list (which may be empty) of the entry points, or *gates*, at which it may be called. The trap handler checks that all inward procedure calls are directed to one of these gates, and generates an error if not. The trap handler also records on a stack the return point and ring number corresponding to the call. Returns across rings are validated against the top of the stack to ensure that a procedure cannot be tricked into returning to a ring lower than that prevailing before the call. The parameters of an inward call also require validation in case they refer to segments which should be protected against the caller.

The disadvantage of hierarchical protection systems such as the one outlined above is that if an object must be accessible in domain $A$ which is not accessible in domain $B$ then $A$ must be higher up the hierarchy than $B$. This implies that everything accessible in $B$ must necessarily be accessible in $A$. This can be regarded as falling a long way short of the goal of giving a process the minimum necessary privileges at all times. However, the various layers of protection do to some extent mirror the layers of construction of an operating system, and therefore form a naturally attractive way of reinforcing operating system structure. The designers of the MULTICS system claim that the hierarchical structure does not in practice impose embarrassing constraints, and that satisfactory protection can be provided. In the next section we shall examine an alternative which does not depend on a hierarchical organisation.

## 9.4 GENERAL SYSTEMS

In the hierarchical protection scheme described above the capabilities which can be exercised by a process are implicit in the number of the ring in which it is executing. Furthermore, transfers of control from one ring to another imply either an extension or a reduction of the capabilities currently available. In a non-hierarchical system, on the other hand, transfers in control between domains are accompanied by quite arbitrary changes in a process's capabilities. The set of capabilities belonging to a process in a particular domain is known as its *capability list*: a change of domain implies a change of capability list. In a hierarchical system the new capability list is always either an extension or subset of the old, while in a non-hierarchical system there is no obvious relationship.

An abstract model for a general protection system (Graham and Denning, 1972) is an *access matrix* (figure 9.4) which denotes the capabilities of various *subjects* for all system *objects* which need protection. A subject is a pair (*process, domain*), so each row in the matrix represents the capability list of a particular process executing in a particular domain. When a process changes domain it becomes a different subject and its capability list is represented by a different row of the access matrix. In general subjects require protection from each other, and so subjects are also regarded as objects.

OBJECTS

| | | Subjects | | | Files | | Devices | |
|---|---|---|---|---|---|---|---|---|
| | $S_1$ | $S_2$ | $S_3$ | $F_1$ | $F_2$ | $D_1$ | $D_2$ | |
| $S_1$ | | stop delete | | read write | | | seek | |
| $S_2$ | | | stop | | update | write | | |
| $S_3$ | | | | delete | execute | | | |
| | | | | | | | | |

(SUBJECTS labels the rows at left)

*Figure 9.4 Part of an access control matrix*

Associated with each object is a *controller* which is entered whenever the object is accessed. Depending on the type of object concerned the controller could be implemented in hardware or software: typical examples might be

| Type of object | Controller |
|---|---|
| file | filing system |
| segment | memory addressing hardware |
| peripheral | device handler |

The controller is responsible for ensuring that a subject possesses the appropriate capability for the type of access requested. A particular protection scheme is characterised by the choice of subjects and objects, by the capabilities denoted by the elements of the access matrix, and by the way in which capabilities can be modified or transferred.

The model includes all the elements of a general protection system, but an efficient implementation for a wide range of object types is difficult to envisage. However, if, as suggested in section 9.2, the range of objects is restricted to memory segments and if a process may change domain only when entering a new segment then implementation can be achieved in terms of the memory addressing hardware. Two approaches to such implementation are described below.

The first approach (Evans and Leclerc, 1967) is to regard a capability, which takes the form (*access indicator, segment base, segment length*), as equivalent to a segment descriptor, and to identify the capability list of a process with its segment table. A change of domain by a process implies a change of segment table. A consequence of this approach is the destruction of the notion of a process-wide address space, since a process will change address space according to the domain in which it is executing. Some difficulties are also encountered in parameter passing: for example, a recursive procedure requires a separate segment table for each level of call, the successive tables giving access to the parameters appropriate to each level.

An alternative approach is that adopted in the Plessey 250 computer (Williams, 1972; England, 1974). We shall describe this implementation in some detail since it illustrates the way in which memory addressing schemes based on capabilities can be expected to some extent to replace the more traditional schemes discussed in chapter 5. (See Fabry, 1974, for strong advocacy of such a development.)

A capability in the Plessey 250 consists of the access indicator, base address and limit address of a particular segment. The capabilities of the current process are held in a set of program accessible processor registers known as *capability registers*, and program addresses are specified by giving the number of a capability register and an offset. The desired memory location is obtained by adding the offset to the base address held in the capability register. The limit address and access indicator are used to check memory and access violations.

The reader might wonder at this point whether the set of capability registers is not conceptually the same thing, apart from differences of speed, as the traditional segment table. The distinction is that the allocation of capability registers is under local program control and the programmer, or compiler, is free to reallocate the registers as he sees fit. By contrast, segment table entries are allocated by an operating system on a global basis, and once allocated they remain fixed.

Since it is economically feasible to provide only a small number of registers, the capabilities of a process are also stored in a capability segment in memory and loaded into the capability registers as required. Thus the capability segment currently accessible to a process represents its capability list and defines its domain of execution. Access privileges 'read capability' and 'write capability', which are distinct from the normal 'read' and 'write' and which apply only to the capability segment, are used to prevent ordinary data items being treated as capabilities. This prevents capabilities being manufactured in data segments and then loaded into capability registers. By convention capability register C(6) is used to address the capability segment of the current process, and register C(7) is used to address the segment containing the code being executed.

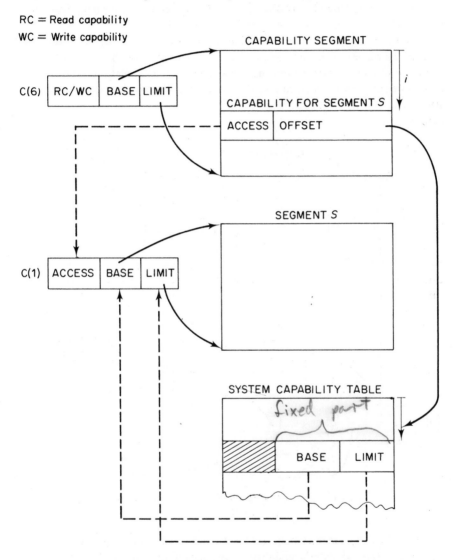

RC = Read capability
WC = Write capability

*Figure 9.5 'Load capability' operation (C(1): = C(6) + i)*

A further refinement is necessary in order to facilitate the sharing of segments among processes. In the scheme as described the relocation in memory of a shared segment would involve a change to the corresponding capabilities in the capability segments of all the processes concerned. To avoid this the base and limit addresses of all segments in memory are contained in a *system capability table*, and all stored capabilities refer to segments individually through this table. Relocation of a segment thus involves an alteration only to the system capability table and not to the entries in the individual capability segments. Figure 9.5 illustrates the process of loading capability register $C(1)$ with a capability for segment $S$ which is contained in the $i$th entry of the capability segment.

It should be noted that the system capability table is itself a segment, addressed by a special capability register, and is accessible only to certain parts of the operating system which are concerned with memory management. It is invisible to all other processes, which can regard the capabilities in the capability segments as pointing directly to the segments concerned.

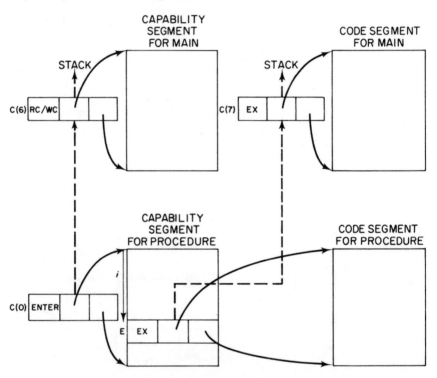

*Figure 9.6 Changing the domain of execution*
*(CALL C(0) + i)*

A process may change domain (that is, change its capability segment) only if it possesses a special 'enter' capability for the capability segment of the new domain. Figure 9.6 illustrates the way in which a process executing a program MAIN calls a procedure SUB in a different domain. Initially $C(6)$ addresses the capability segment for MAIN and $C(7)$ holds an 'execute' capability for the segment containing the program code of MAIN. The process possesses in $C(0)$ an 'enter' capability for the capability segment of SUB, which in turn contains in its $i$th location an 'execute' capability E for the code segment of SUB. A procedure call specifying C(0) and offset *i* results in C(6) being replaced by the 'enter' capability in C(0), and C(7) by the 'execute' capability E. Thus C(6) and C(7) now point to the appropriate capability and code segments in the new domain. A 'read capability' privilege is added to C(6) to enable the called procedure to read its own capabilities, and the previous values of C(6) and C(7) are placed on a stack for retrieval on the subsequent return. Neither the caller nor the called procedure have access to each other's capabilities, except for those capabilities which may be passed as parameters in registers C(1) to C(5). The scheme therefore affords complete protection between mutually suspicious procedures.

## 9.5 CONCLUSION

We have seen in this chapter that the need for protection is a natural consequence of a multi-user environment. With the advent of large scale data bases and a growing concern over privacy, security and reliability, this need is likely to become more pressing. Although protection has traditionally been provided, to a greater or lesser extent, by a variety of mechanisms at various points in the system it is now becoming possible to take an integrated approach. Given suitable hardware we would wish to include in our paper operating system a protection scheme similar to one of those described above.

# 10 *Reliability*

In section 2.3 we stated that one of the desirable features of an operating system is reliability; indeed, an unreliable system is of very little use. In this chapter we examine more closely what is meant by reliability, and discuss ways in which the reliability of an operating system can be increased. We shall see that reliability is . not an 'add-on extra', but a requirement which must be considered from the earliest stages of system design.

## 10.1 OBJECTIVES AND TERMINOLOGY

It will be apparent from the preceding chapters that an operating system is a complex piece of software which is expected to perform a variety of functions for a diverse set of users. It is important to the users that these functions are performed correctly, and one of the principal objectives of the system designer is to ensure that this is the case. The task of the designer is made more difficult in that the finished product will not be operating in a perfect world: it is likely to be subjected to a large variety of circumstances which could adversely affect its functioning. Such circumstances include malfunction of the hardware of the host computer, errors in procedure by the computer operators, and illegal or meaningless requests supplied by the user. An operating system should continue providing service, possibly of a degraded nature, even in the face of such adverse circumstances.

These remarks lead us to define the *reliability* of an operating system as the degree to which it meets its specifications in respect of service to its users, even when subjected to unexpected and hostile conditions. This definition emphasises that reliability is a relative rather than an absolute concept: no system can be totally reliable since, to take an extreme example, it would be impossible to provide service in the face of the simultaneous failure of all hardware components of the computer. A highly reliable operating system will continue to meet its specifications even under great pressure from hardware malfunction or user error, a less reliable system may depart from its specifications when subjected only to a single meaningless request.

The level of reliability which should be achieved by an operating system depends, of course, on the reliance its users place on it. Heavy reliance, as in a system which controls a space capsule or monitors the condition of hospital patients, demands high reliability; lesser reliance, as in a system for document preparation and retrieval, requires less reliability. Since (as we shall see later) high reliability often incurs high costs, the system designer should aim at a level of reliability which is commensurate with the reliance of the users. (It is interesting to note, however, that the reliance of users may be influenced by the reliability of the system.)

The concept of reliability should not be confused with that of *correctness*: the notions are related but distinct. An operating system is *correct* if when running in a a specified environment it exhibits a specified (desired) behaviour. Correctness is certainly a desirable attribute of an operating system, but it is an insufficient condition for reliability. This is because demonstrations of correctness, whether by testing or formal proof, rely on assumptions about the environment which are generally invalid. Such assumptions typically concern the nature of inputs and the correct functioning of hardware, and may be quite unjustified in practice. Putting it another way, the environment in which a system operates rarely matches that which is assumed in the demonstration of correctness.

Correctness is not only an insufficient condition for reliability, but, perhaps more surprisingly, it is also an unnecessary one. Parts of an operating system may be incorrect in that the algorithms governing particular processes may not produce the required effect, but the system can still operate reliably. As an example, consider a filing system in which the *close* routine in some circumstances omits to record the length of a file in the corresponding directory entry. Provided that the file terminates with a recognisable 'end of file' mark, the I/O routines can still read the file successfully, and the system will perform reliably even in the face of the incorrect operation of one of its components. This example illustrates the use of redundant, or superfluous, information to conceal and recover from errors, a technique to which we shall return later.

The reader should not assume from this that correctness is unimportant. It may be neither a necessary nor a sufficient condition for reliability, but it certainly helps. An operating system which is correct is likely to be more reliable than one which is not. It would be bad practice indeed for a designer to depend on reliability mechanisms to conceal the effects of known deficiencies, or even to justify lack of effort towards achieving correctness. The proper course is to attempt to produce a system which is correct with respect to specified assumptions about the environment, and at the same time to design reliability mechanisms to cater for those occasions on which the assumptions are invalid. We shall examine these complementary approaches in later sections.

At this point we introduce three more items of terminology. We define an *error* to be a deviation of the system from its specified behaviour. Thus an error is an event; examples are the allocation of an unsharable resource to two processes, or the deletion of the directory entry for a file which is still being used. An error may be caused by a hardware malfunction, by the unanticipated action of a user or operator, or by a deficiency ('bug') in one of the programs within the system. In all cases we use the term *fault* to mean the cause of an error. When an error occurs it is probable that some items of information within the system are corrupted. We refer to such corruption as the *damage* caused by the error; damage can of course result in faults which lead to further errors. We shall see that one of the means of achieving high reliability is to limit the damage that can be caused by an error, and hence limit the propagation of errors throughout the system.

From the foregoing discussion we can see that efforts toward producing a highly reliable operating system should be concentrated on the following areas:

(a) *fault avoidance*: elimination of faults in the design and implementation stages; that is, production of a correct system.
(b) *error detection*: detection of errors as soon as possible in order to reduce the damage caused.
(c) *fault treatment*: identification and elimination of any fault which produces an error.
(d) *error recovery*: assessment and repair of the damage resulting from an error.

In the following sections we shall deal with each of these in turn.


## 10.2 FAULT AVOIDANCE

As we have seen, faults in a computer system may stem from the hardware, from operator or user incompetence and ignorance, or from 'bugs' in the software. Ways of avoiding each of these types of fault are discussed below.


### (1) Operator and User Faults

We shall say little about operator and user generated faults other than that they can never be eliminated: all that can be hoped for is a reduction in their number by means of appropriate training and user education programmes.


### (2) Hardware Faults

The most obvious way of reducing the incidence of hardware faults is to use the most reliable components which can be obtained within the overall cost constraints. Hardware designers use several methods of enhancing reliability, ranging from the obvious — using individually reliable components — to more complex techniques which incorporate some form of error detection and recovery within each subsystem. Error detection is usually based on the recording or transmission of redundant information, such as parity bits and checksums; recovery is often attempted by repeating the operation which gave rise to the error. Examples of this technique are magnetic tape and disc drives which are designed to repeat operations a limited number of times if either parity or checksum errors occur. Retrying operations is of course useful only for transient faults (that is, faults which are due to temporary conditions such as interference or dust particles); permanent faults will still result in errors.

Another technique which is often used in data transmission is the use of error detecting and correcting codes, in which redundant information transmitted with the data provides a means of recovery from certain transmission errors. Yet another technique is that of *majority polling*, in which several (usually three) identical components are supplied with the same inputs and their outputs are compared. If the outputs differ the majority verdict is taken to be correct, and the component producing the minority verdict is noted as being suspect. A component which is repeatedly in the minority is assumed to be faulty and can be replaced. Majority polling is an expensive reliability technique since it relies on replication of components and it is normally used only when really high reliability is essential.

The aim of all the techniques discussed is to *mask* the hardware faults from the software which runs on it. That is, faults may be present in the hardware but their effects are concealed from the software, so that as far as the software is concerned the hardware appears fault free. We shall see in section 10.6 that the notion of masking can be extended into the operating system itself, so that errors which occur in one level of the system are hidden from the levels outside it.

## (3) Software Faults

There are several complementary approaches to reducing the incidence of software faults. We discuss three of the principal ones below.

The first approach is to adopt management practices, programming methodologies and software tools which are a positive aid towards producing a fault free product. In the mid 1960s it was believed in some quarters that the larger the piece of software to be produced the more programmers should be assigned to it. IBM's experience with huge armies of programmers on OS/360 exploded this myth, and it is now realised that indiscriminate application of manpower is likely to create more problems than it solves. The grouping of programmers into small teams, popularly known as 'chief programmer teams', is now considered a better way of organising software production. Each team is responsible for a module of software which has precisely defined external specifications and interfaces, and within the team each member has a well defined function, such as coding, documentation, or liaison with other teams. Detailed consideration of such organisational practices is beyond our present scope: a revealing and entertaining account of various pitfalls is given by Brooks (1975).

The way in which programmers actually go about writing programs can have considerable influence on the quality of the finished product, in terms of coherence, comprehensibility and freedom from faults. Several programming methodologies have been advocated during the last few years, the most widely known being *structured programming* (Dahl *et al.*, 1972; Wirth, 1971) and its various derivatives (for example, Yourdon, 1975; Jackson, 1975). Structured programming has been sufficiently publicised elsewhere for us not to go into detail here: the reader who wishes to know more is referred to the accounts above, or to Alagic and Arbib (1978).

The software tools which are of most help in creating a fault free product are probably an editor, a macro-assembler, and a compiler for a suitable high-level language. We have already remarked in section 4.2 that the only parts of an operating system which need to be written in assembly language are those which are intimately bound up with the host hardware, namely parts of the nucleus and the I/O device handlers. The use of a high-level language for the rest of the system speeds up the production of useful code and facilitates the elimination of faults. It is sometimes said that high-level languages are unsuitable for writing operating systems since the object code produced is less efficient in execution than the corresponding hand-written code. There are at least three counters to this view: first, that a good optimising compiler can often produce better code than a good assembly language programmer; second, that areas of residual inefficiency can if necessary be optimised by hand; and third, that reliability is at least as important a goal as efficiency.

The second general approach to reducing the incidence of software faults is to attempt to prove, by more or less formal means, that all programs in the operating system, and all their interactions, are correct. This is a formidable task, which for large systems is beyond the current state of the art. However, pioneering work by Floyd (1967), Hoare (1972), and Dijkstra (1976) has opened up the possibility of such proofs being possible in the not too distant future. Even now, a great deal of confidence in the correctness of a system can be inspired by proofs of correctness of some of its component programs.

The most popular approach to proving program correctness (Alagic and Arib, 1978; Hantler and King, 1976) is to formulate assertions (usually expressed in predicate calculus) which are to be true at various stages of program execution. The proof then proceeds inductively from the assumption of the initial assertion to verification that execution of the program statements does indeed make the subsequent assertions true. The chief difficulties encountered are the formulation of appropriate assertions, and the rather laborious step by step proof of their truth.

The third approach to eliminating software faults is by means of systematic testing. Testing has always been a prime method of detecting faults, but there is surprisingly little agreement on an appropriate methodology. Ideally, one would like to test a program on all possible inputs, but this is clearly impractical; all one can hope for is that the test data chosen will reveal all remaining faults. There is no general way of selecting test data to do this, though several pragmatic guidelines have been proposed. One such guideline is to select data which will exercise all possible paths through a program. Another is to select data which lie at the extremes of the allowable ranges: for example, zero is an obvious choice in any situation where the inputs can range over the positive integers.

The difficulty of testing is compounded when a large number of programs are to be executed by several interacting processes, as is the case in an operating system. Not only must each program be tested, but so must the interfaces between different programs and processes. The only hope of doing this at all successfully is to keep the interfaces as simple as possible.

We can summarise this discussion by saying that none of the approaches outlined above — programming methodology, formal correctness proofs, and testing — can be relied on to yield a fault free product. The techniques are still evolving, but it is fair to say that a combination of the three approaches can even now substantially raise one's confidence in the correctness of the software produced.

## 10.3 ERROR DETECTION

The key to error detection is *redundancy* — that is, the provision of 'superfluous' information which can be used to check the validity of the 'main' information contained within the system. The term 'redundancy' reflects the fact that the information used for checking is redundant as far as the main algorithms of the system are concerned. We have already seen in the last section how redundant information such as party bits and checksums can be used for error detection in the hardware sphere. Coding is also a useful means of error detection, and in some cases can be used for recovery as well. As mentioned before, errors detected by the hardware may be masked by the hardware itself, or they may be reported to the operating system by means of traps into the first level interrupt handler (section 4.4). Examples of the latter type of error are arithmetic overflow, memory violation, and protection violation. The actions which can be taken by the operating system in such cases will be described later in this chapter.

Error detection may also be undertaken by the operating system itself. A common form of checking is for processes to check the consistency of the data structures they use. An example of this might be for the processor queue to be held as a doubly linked list and for the scheduler to trace the links both forwards and backwards wherever it accesses the queue. The redundant information provided in this case is the set of backward links: only the forward ones are required for the main scheduling and dispatching algorithms. Another example is the checking of table modifications by maintaining in the table a checksum of all its entries. When an entry is modified the effect on the checksum can be predicted by calculation. If the checksum after modification does not correspond to that predicted then an error has occurred during modification.

A generalisation of this form of checking (Randell, 1975) is to associate with each major action of a process an *acceptance test* which can be used as a criterion of whether the action has been properly performed. The acceptance test is a Boolean expression which is evaluated (as part of the process execution) after the action is completed. If the result is 'true' the action is considered to have been performed correctly; if it is 'false' an error has occurred. The acceptance test can be as stringent as deemed necessary; it will be formulated to check for those errors which the designer feels are most probable. As an example consider the action of the scheduler in periodically modifying process priorities and re-ordering the processor queue. The acceptance test for this operation may be simply that the process descriptors in the re-ordered queue are indeed in priority order. A more stringent acceptance test contains the additional constraint that the number of descriptors in the queue is the same as before, thus guarding against the inadvertent detachment or duplication of a descriptor. There is of course usually a trade-off between the stringency of an acceptance test and the overhead of performing it, a trade-off which applies to all error detection mechanisms. The designer must weigh the costs, in capital equipment or performance degradation, against the benefits accruing. Unfortunately, it is often the case that neither costs nor benefits can be accurately measured.

So far we have dealt only with errors which occur within a single hardware or software component. Errors which occur at the interfaces between components are more difficult to detect, but some advantage can be gained from checking the credibility of any information passed across an interface. For example, some procedure parameters can be checked to see that they fall within an appropriate range, and it may be possible to check that messages passed between processes conform to some established protocol.

We conclude this section by noting that early detection of an error is the best way of limiting the damage which may be caused, and of limiting the wasted processing which may result. The capability of an operating system to react to errors soon after they occur can be greatly enhanced by the provision of suitable hardware protection mechanisms. Thus the protection mechanisms discussed in chapter 9 can make an important contribution not only to the security of an operating system but also to its reliability. (See Denning, 1976 for greater elaboration of this point.)

## 10.4 FAULT TREATMENT

Treatment of a fault first involves its location, and then its repair. As any systems programmer will testify, detection of an error and location of the corresponding fault are not at all the same thing. An error may have several possible causes, located in either the hardware or the software, and none of them may be apparent. One of the main aids to fault identification is the detection of errors before their cause is obscured by consequent damage and further errors. Thus the early detection of errors, as indicated at the end of section 10.3, is of prime importance.

In some cases it may be possible to take the easy option of ignoring the fault altogether, but this involves assumptions about the frequency of the errors it can cause and the extent of their damage. For example, it may not be considered worthwhile to attempt to locate a transient hardware fault until the frequency of errors it causes crosses some threshold of unacceptability (Avizienis, 1977). Usually, however, it is important that a fault be located and dealt with. The search for a fault will generally be directed by the investigator's understanding of the system structure. If this is incomplete, or if the fault has affected the structure, then the investigator's task is difficult indeed.

One way of helping the investigator is for the system to produce a trace, or log, of its recent activity. Events recorded in the log might be process activations, procedure entries, I/O transfers, and so on. Unfortunately the amount and detail of information recorded must be very large if the log is to be of practical value, and the overhead of recording it can be very high. Some advantage can perhaps be gained from making the trace optional, so that it need be switched on only when there is reason to believe that the system is malfunctioning. It is also worth while making the trace selective, so that only those parts of the system which are suspect need log their activities. This of course requires a subjective judgement, itself prone to error, of which are the suspect parts.

Once a fault has been located its treatment involves some form of repair. In the case of hardware faults repair usually comprises the replacement of a faulty component. This may be done manually or automatically, depending on the ability of the hardware to locate its own faults and 'switch out' a faulty component. Manual replacement may involve taking the entire system out of service for a time, or, preferably, it may proceed in parallel with continued service, possibly at a degraded level. Repair of a disc drive, for example, should not interrupt normal service if other drives are available, but replacement of a printed circuit board in the central processor of a single CPU system will probably require a complete shutdown and restart.

Faults in software components arise from deficiencies in design and implementation, or from corruption caused by previous errors. (Unlike hardware, software does not suffer from faults due to ageing.) Removal of a design or implementation fault usually involves the replacement of a (hopefully small) number of lines of program, while a corrupted program can be replaced by a backup copy held elsewhere. The repair of corrupted data is a topic we shall leave to the next section, which deals with error recovery generally. As with hardware, one would hope that software components can be replaced without the need to close down the entire system, and the system should be designed with this in mind.

## 10.5 ERROR RECOVERY

Recovery from an error involves assessment of the damage which has been caused, followed by an attempt to repair it. Damage assessment may be based entirely on *a priori* reasoning by the investigator, or it may involve the system itself in performing a number of checks to determine what damage has occurred. In either case, assessment (like fault identification) will be guided by assumed causal relationships defined by the system structure. An error in updating a file directory can, for example, be expected to damage the filing system but not the process structure or the device descriptors. There is of course a danger that the system structure, and hence any assumed relationship, will itself be damaged, but the probability of this happening is greatly reduced if appropriate hardware protection mechanisms are employed (as suggested in section 10.3).

The usual approach to repairing damage is to back up the affected processes to a state which existed before the error occurred. This approach relies on the provision of *recovery points* (or *checkpoints*) at which sufficient information is recorded about the state of a process to allow it to be reinstated later if necessary. The information required is at least the volatile environment and a copy of the process descriptor; it may also include a copy of the content of the memory space used by the process. The interval between recovery points determines the amount of processing which is likely to be lost when an error occurs. The loss of information after an error can be reduced by *audit-trail* techniques, in which all modifications to the process state are logged as they occur. Error recovery then consists of backing up to the last recovery point and then making the state changes indicated by the audit log. Audit-trail techniques are analogous to the incremental dump of a file system, described in section 7.5; in fact the incremental dump can be viewed as a particular audit-trail mechanism.

Recovery points and audit-trails imply the recording of all state information and all modifications to it. An interesting alternative (Randell, 1975) is the *recovery block* scheme, in which the only state information recorded is that which is actually modified. Since the scheme also includes elements of error detection and fault treatment we feel it is worthy of brief description.

A recovery block is a section of program with the following structure

**ensure**      *acceptance test* **by**
              *primary alternate*
**elseby**          .
              *secondary alternate*
**elseby**
              *other alternate*
**elseby**          .
  .            .
  .            .
  .

The primary alternate is the program fragment which is normally executed; the other alternates are used only if the primary alternate fails. Success or failure of an alternate is determined by execution of the acceptance test (see section 10.3) associated with the block. Thus execution of the recovery block first involves execution of the primary alternate, followed by execution of the acceptance test. If the test passes, which is the normal case, the entire block is deemed to have been executed successfully. If the test fails, the process state is restored to that which existed before the primary alternate was executed, and the secondary alternate is then executed. The acceptance test is again used to determine success or failure, and further alternates are invoked as necessary. If all alternates fail then the block as a whole is said to fail, and recovery has to be made by invoking an alternate block if there is one (recovery blocks may be nested to any depth), or by restarting the process if not.

The alternates within a recovery block can be viewed as software spares which are automatically utilised whenever the primary alternate fails. Unlike hardware spares the alternates are not of identical design, and usually employ different algorithms. The primary alternate employs the most efficient or otherwise desirable algorithm for fulfilling the function of the block; the other alternates employ less efficient algorithms, or algorithms which fulfil the desired function in only a partial, but still tolerable, fashion. Failure of an alternate is regarded as an exceptional occurrence (akin to an error due to a transient hardware fault), and the alternate is replaced only for the current execution of the block. It is wise, however, to log all failures, so that residual design and programming faults can be recognised and eliminated.

The recovery block scheme relies for its operation on the ability to restore a process state whenever an acceptance test fails. The ease of doing this depends on whether or not the process concerned has interacted with other processes during execution of the block. If it has not, restoration of its state reduces to restoring the prior values of all program variables and registers which have been changed. This can be effected by means of a 'recovery cache' (Horning *et al.*, 1974), a portion of memory in which values are stored before being modified. Only those values which are modified need be stored in the cache, and values which are modified several times need be stored only once. Failure of an alternate causes the restoration of values from the cache before the next alternate is tried; success of an alternate leads to the deletion of values from the cache, since the modifications can now be regarded as valid. The nesting of recovery blocks is catered for by organising the cache in a manner similar to a stack.

The case of process interaction within a recovery block is more difficult to handle. A possible approach (Randell, 1975) is to regard any interaction between two processes as a 'conversation' between them. If one of the processes has to be backed up during a conversation then so must the other, since the information transmitted in the conversation may have been erroneous. Thus neither process may proceed beyond the end of a conversation until both have passed acceptance tests at its conclusion, and failure of either acceptance test results in the backup of both processes to the start of the conversation. The idea can be extended to simultaneous conversations between several processes.

This description of the recovery block scheme has been necessarily brief, but the reader will recognise that it combines several aspects of fault tolerance discussed earlier. Error detection is achieved by means of the acceptance tests; fault treatment is effected by the provision of alternates; and recovery is based on the cache mechanism. A more detailed description of the scheme is given in the quoted references.

## 10.6 MULTILEVEL ERROR HANDLING

In the previous few sections we have described various error handling techniques. In this section we suggest how these techniques can be incorporated into the layered structure of our paper operating system.

The principal aim is to mask from each level of the operating system the errors which occur at levels below it. Thus each level of the system is to be as far as possible responsible for its own error recovery, so that to levels above it appears fault free. The idea is an extension into the operating system of the hardware error masking discussed in section 10.2. In cases where masking is impossible, errors in a lower level which occur while performing some function for a higher level should be reported to the higher level in an orderly fashion (for example, by a specific error return). The higher level may itself then be able to perform some kind of recovery, thus masking the error from higher levels still. Those errors which cannot be masked at any level must, of course, eventually be reported to either the user or the operator. At the lowest level of the system, errors which are detected by the CPU hardware, but cannot be masked, are reported to the nucleus by means of error traps into the first level interrupt handler (section 4.4).

As an example of what we mean, consider a user process which wishes to open a file. The process invokes the filing system by calling the *open* routine (section 7.6), which in turn invokes the I/O system by calling the DOIO procedure (section 6.2) to read the user directory from disc. The required I/O transfer is eventually initiated by the disc device handler. In the event of a parity error a first level of masking may be provided by the hardware of the disc controller itself, which is probably designed to detect such an error and re-read the corresponding block. If a few retries fail to correct the situation the error will be reported to the device handler by means of the device status register, which is set by the controller at the end of the transfer. The device handler may attempt to mask the error by re-initiating the entire operation, but if this is unsuccessful the error must be reported back to the *open* routine in the filing system (by means of an error return from DOIO). Within the filing system recovery is possible if another copy of the directory exists elsewhere: the I/O system can be requested to read the backup copy. If for some reason this also fails, or if the filing system is not sufficiently well designed to maintain backup directories, then the error can be masked no longer and must be reported to the user.

Another error which could occur during the file opening operation is the corruption of a queue pointer in the disc device request queue. This may be due to hardware malfunction or to a programming fault. If, as suggested in section 10.3, the queue is organised as a doubly linked list and the queue manipulation routines trace both forward and backward links, then loss of the IORB for the directory transfer can be avoided. Damage to the pointer is repaired by the queue manipulation routines themselves, thus masking the error from the device handler and hence from the filing system and the user process.

By contrast it is interesting to note what will probably happen if the request queue is only singly linked, so that the queue manipulation routines cannot detect the error, let alone mask it. In this case the IORB will become detached from the queue, and the value of the semaphore *request pending* (section 6.2) will be inconsistent with the number of requests in the queue. One of two things will happen next. The first possibility is that the device handler will assume that a successful *wait* operation on *request pending* implies the existence of an IORB in the queue. It will then remove a non-existent IORB from the queue, interpret the resulting garbage as a valid I/O request, and provoke untold further errors. The other possibility is that the device handler will check that the request queue does indeed contain at least one valid IORB and, finding that it does not, will report this fact back to the DOIO procedure. In this case the error will have been successfully masked from the user, since the IORB can be regenerated. The lesson, however, is to include as much error detection and recovery capability as possible at each level, thus avoiding the potential of serious damage. Further examples of multilevel error handling along these lines are given in a description of the reliability mechanisms of the HYDRA system (Wulf, 1975).

Some errors, of course, should not be masked, since they are indicative of a gross fault in a user program. These errors are not system errors, but user errors: the operating system's responsibility is to do no more than report them to the user. An example is arithmetic overflow, which is detected by the processor and reported to the system nucleus via the first level interrupt handler. The interrupt routine in the nucleus can readily identify the culprit as the current process for the processor concerned, and the process can be aborted with an appropriate error message. (It can be argued that masking of arithmetic overflow is possible, for example, by setting the affected location to the largest representable number. However, we consider such action to be undesirable, since it is likely to lead to further errors which will obscure the original fault.) Other errors which should not be masked are memory and protection violations resulting from execution of user programs. The latter could, however, be logged, since they may be indicative of deliberate attempts to break down system security.

## 10.7 CONCLUSION

In this chapter we have described techniques for enhancing the reliability of an operating system. As computers intrude into many more areas of human activity, and as reliance on them increases, reliability will be of paramount importance. The techniques we have described, although still subject to considerable refinement, form a basis for achieving the reliability required. As far as our paper operating system is concerned, we note that its layered structure is well suited to the multilevel error handling suggested in section 10.6, and that we therefore expect, by using the techniques described, to achieve high reliability.

Finally, we refer the reader who wishes to make a more detailed study of reliability to the excellent surveys by Denning (1976), Randell *et al.* (1978) and Kopetz (1979).

# 11 *Job Control*

In the preceding chapters we have described how a large scale job-shop operating system can be constructed. At present our operating system exists somewhat in a vacuum since we have not yet specified how we can inform it about the jobs we want it to do. The next step is to manufacture an interface between the user and the operating system so that the user can tell the system what he requires of it. The interface can also be used to present information, such as resource requirements, about each job so that the system can optimise performance in the ways described earlier. Of course communication between user and system is not all in one direction; we must also construct a complementary interface by which the system can tell the user what it has been doing.

## 11.1 SOME GENERAL REMARKS

The interface between user and system implies the provision of a language, however primitive, in which communication can take place. The nature of the language is heavily dependent on the type of operating system concerned; languages for multi-access use often differ widely from those used in batch systems. The reason for this is that the interactive nature of multi-access working allows a user the opportunity to direct the course of his work in person, and to respond to system actions as they happen. In a batch system, on the other hand, once the user has submitted his job he has no further control over it. Hence he must give explicit instructions in advance as to what course of action is to be followed, possibly specifying alternatives in cases where he cannot foresee precisely what eventualities may occur.

A consequence of the two styles of working is that languages used for batch operation tend to be more complex and more powerful than those used in multi-access. Indeed in the latter case the language may be no more than a set of commands which can be used as directives to the operating system. Such a language is often termed a *command language*, as opposed to the more general *job control language* used in a batch environment. Some operating systems, such as VME/B on the ICL 2900 range of computers, attempt to provide both batch and multi-access control in a single language. In these cases multi-access users usually find themselves employing only a subset of the complete job control language.

```
                                              Notes
. LOG                                          (1)

USER# 2167,2167

PASSWORD:                                      (2)

LOGGED ON AT 15.39 5 MAY 74

. EX PROG.ALG                                  (3)

ALGOL:PROG

        ERROR AT LINE 3
        UNDECLARED IDENTIFIER

EXIT

. EDIT PROG.ALG                                (4)

        editing commands terminating with EXIT

. EX                                           (5)

ALGOL:PROG

        NO ERRORS

EXIT

LOADER 5K CORE

EXECUTION

        user types any data for program;
        results of execution typed out

END OF EXECUTION    1.26 SECS

. KJOB                                         (6)

LOGGED OFF USER 2167,2167 at 15:54

RUNTIME = 2.18   CONNECT TIME = 15:10

.
```

*Figure 11.1 Example terminal session. Notes: (1) request to log on; (2) echoing of password is suppressed; (3) compile and execute program in previously created file PROG.ALG; (4) edit program; (5) compile and execute same program; (6) log off*

A common desirable feature of both command and job control languages is that they should be easy to use. We shall say more about this later.


## 11.2 COMMAND LANGUAGES

The example in figure 11.1, loosely based on the DEC System-10 multi-access monitor, illustrates several points which should be borne in mind when designing a command language. The example is the record of a short terminal session; responses typed by the system have been underlined to distinguish them from commands typed by the user. The figures in parentheses refer to the explanatory notes.

Points arising from the example are

(1)    To avoid unnecessary typing, sensible abbreviations should be allowed wherever possible (for example, LOG and EX are abbreviations of LOGON and EXECUTE respectively). The full command can be typed whenever the user is unsure of a particular abbreviation.

(2)    Commands should preferably be mnemonic, so that they are easy to remember and easy to guess at if forgotten (for example LOGON, EXECUTE and EDIT).

(3)    In commands which take parameters defaults should be supplied whenever sensible (for example in the EXECUTE command the default file name is the name of the file used last time; the default I/O device during execution is the terminal). The judicious choice of defaults can save a lot of tedious typing.

(4)    It should be possible to perform commonplace activities with very little effort. (EXECUTE is a single command which causes the compilation, loading, and execution of the named file.)

(5)    A sensible set of conventions can reduce the typing load. (A file whose name has ALG as its second component is recognised as an Algol program.)

(6)    The format of commands should be as free as possible (for example the number of spaces between the command elements is arbitrary).

(7)    It should always be obvious whether or not the system is ready to receive another command (this is signified by the dot at the beginning of each line).

(8)    The system should give sufficient information to the user to indicate what is happening, but not so much that he is drowned in verbiage.

We shall not dwell further on command languages except to note that many of the points above are also applicable to job control languages.


## 11.3 JOB CONTROL LANGUAGES

In early batch operating systems, such as the IBSYS system for the IBM 7090 series, job control was achieved by the insertion of *control cards* at various points in the program and data. The control cards had some particular identifying feature (in IBSYS a '$' in column 1) and were interpreted by the operating system as instructions as to what to do with the cards which followed. The disadvantages of this arrangement are threefold.

(1)     The sequence of operations to be performed cannot be altered in the light of the success or failure of previous steps.
(2)     Control information is scattered throughout the input, which is logically unappealing and renders it prone to error.
(3)     The control cards need some special combination of characters to identify them; this combination must therefore never occur in programs or data. (One way round this restriction is to provide a special control statement which alters the identifying feature for all subsequent control cards to some other combination of characters. This option is available in OS/360 JCL.)

In some systems (for example DEC System-10 batch) this type of job control still persists. However, many systems, following Atlas, require that all job control information should be located in a *job description* at the start of a job. The job description is effectively a program written in a job control language which controls the passage of the job through the computing system.

The control information to be specified in a job description can be classified as follows.

## (1) Accounting Information

This usually consists of the job name and the user identity. The latter can be checked against the list of bona fide users in the accounting file, and any charge-able resources used by the job can be debited against the corresponding account.

## (2) Scheduling Information

This generally consists of a specification of the maximum amounts of various resources which the job will use. Systems such as OS/360, where jobs are broken up into separate job steps, may require resource specifications for each step. The information required is that which can be used by the scheduler for (a) deciding which job to start next, (b) allocating priorities, (c) avoiding deadlock, and (d) terminating jobs which exceed their resource limits. Typical resource specifications will include memory occupancy, processor time, and output limits.

Other scheduling information that might be included is a request that the job have a certain priority, or a requirement that the job be run after some other job. Sequencing specifications like this are useful in cases when a job is dependent on a file left by some other job.

## (3) I/O Information

This is the information used in stream based systems to associate streams with physical I/O devices (the reader who wishes to remind himself about streams should refer to section 6.1). In non-stream systems this section of the job description is used to request the assignment of I/O devices for the job. Specifications of character codes and block size may also be included under this heading.

## (4) Procedural Information

This part of the job description actually tells the operating system what the user requires it to do. Some job control languages may allow nothing more than a simple sequence of directives; others may provide facilities for branching on the result of a previous step.

In some job control languages, notably that for Atlas, these four kinds of information are easily distinguished; in others, such as OS/360 JCL, they are intermingled in the same statements. Examples of three languages are given in figures 11.2, 11.3 and 11.4. Figure 11.2 shows a job description in a simple language loosely based on the Atlas style; figures 11.3 and 11.4 (due to B. Shearing) show job descriptions for the same Fortran compile and go job written in GEORGE job control language and OS/360 JCL respectively.

```
                                      Notes

   JOB AML123 SAMPLE          job header and accounting
                              information

   CORE 15 PAGES 25       ⎫
                          ⎬  scheduling information
   TIME  200              ⎪

   AFTER AML123 SORT      ⎭

   INPUT 1 = CDR          ⎫
                          ⎪  I/O information.  Quotes used to
   INPUT 2 = 'MYDATA'     ⎬  distinguish file names from
                          ⎪  device names
   OUTPUT 1 = LPT         ⎭

   COMPILE FORTRAN        ⎫  procedural information.  File
                          ⎬  name for the compiled program
   EXECUTE                ⎭  supplied by default

   END

        program cards

   ****                       job terminator
```

*Figure 11.2 Atlas-style job description*

The conditional branching capabilities of GEORGE are in fact considerably more powerful than the example illustrates; it is possible to test for various messages output by programs and to jump forwards or backwards in the job description. Conditional branches in OS/360 are implemented by leaving certain condition codes in an accumulator at the end of each job step (note 6 in the example), but tests on these codes can result only in limited forward jumps.

```
                              Notes

    JOB FORTGO, AML              header and accounting
                                 information

    FORTRAN *CRO T1              compile from card reader
                                 zero

    LOAD T1                      object program from file T1

    ASSIGN *CRO                  I/O requests

    ASSIGN *LPO                  asterisk distinguishes
                                 devices from files

    TIME 2 SECS

    ENTER

    IF FAIL, GO TO 10            conditional branch

    ENDJOB

    10 LISTFILE MONITOR, *LPO    trace listing

    ENDJOB
```

*Figure 11.3 GEORGE job description*

The observant reader will have noticed that the job description in figure 11.3 is far simpler than that in figure 11.4. To some extent this is due to the rigid format (label, statement type, parameters) used in OS/360, and also to the obscure origin of many of the symbols and abbreviations. However, the main reason for the disparity is the use in figure 11.3 of a job description *macro*. The line FORTRAN *CRO T1 is expanded by the job description interpreter into a sequence of statements (91 lines in all!) which specify in detail the actions to be taken during compilation, particularly in the event of various kinds of failure. This is an example of a feature which appears in most job control languages and which can greatly reduce the effort of writing job descriptions. Any sequence of job control statements which are frequently used can be stored as a macro within the system; the user may call the macro with the parameters appropriate to his particular job. (In the example the parameters of the FORTRAN macro are the device names or file names for the source and object programs.) In OS/360 a macro is called a catalog procedure; the job description in figure 11.4 can in fact be rewritten in a much shorter form if a suitable catalog procedure has been defined. The expansion of the macros and the substitution of parameters is performed by the job description interpreter before the job runs; the mechanism is the same as that used by an assembler.

The macro feature can be even more useful if users are allowed to define their own macros for jobs which they run frequently but which are not provided for by the system library.

```
                                                                   Notes

//FORTGO    JOB    (09,437,35), AML                                  (1)

//COMP      EXEC   PGM=IEYFORT, PARM='SOURCE'                        (2)

//SYSPRINT  DD     SYSOUT=A                                          (3)

//SYSLIN    DD     DSNAME=SYSL.UT4, DISP=OLD                         (4)
                   DCB=(RECFM=FB,LRECL=80, BLKSIZE=800)


//SYSIN     DD     *                                                 (5)

            Fortran program

//GO        EXEC   PGM=FORTLINK, COND=(4,LT, COMP)
                                                                     (6)

//SYSPRINT  DD     SYSOUT=A

//SYSLIN    DD     DSNAME=*.COMP.SYSLIN, DISP=OLD


//SYSLIB    DD     DSNAME=SYSL.FORTLIB,DISP=OLD                      (7)

//FT03F001  DD     SYSOUT=A, DCB=(RECFM=FA, BLKSIZE=133)


//FT05F001  DD     DDNAME=SYSIN

//FT06F001  DD     SYSOUT=A, DCB=(RECFM=FA, BLKSIZE=133)


//FT07F001  DD     UNIT=SYSCP

//GO.SYSIN  DD     *

            data cards
```

*Figure 11.4 OS/360 job description. Notes: (1) header
and accounting information; (2) execute
Fortran compiler; (3) listing to printer;
(4) specifies where object program is to go;
(5) input to compiler follows; (6) execute
linking loader if condition code left by
step COMP is less than 4 (no compilation
errors); (7) call for Fortran library*

It is evident that the inclusion of conditional statements and macros makes job control languages increasingly similar to high level programming languages. There seems to be no reason why job control languages should not progress even further in this direction and incorporate such features as loops, compound statements, and procedures which can be called at job run time. This high level language approach has in fact been adopted in job control on the MU5 computer (Frank, 1976) and on the ICL 2900 series.

A further development which can be expected is the inclusion of facilities for specifying that various parts of a job may be run in parallel. Such information could be used by the scheduler to initiate a job as a set of processes running in parallel rather than in sequence. The advent of multi-processor systems, in which real gains can be made by parallelism, will perhaps provide the incentive to bring this development about.

Another possible development lies in pursuing the analogy with high level programming languages by introducing job control languages which can be compiled or interpreted on any system. This would constitute a significant advance towards machine independence in running jobs; at present the machine independence gained at the programming level is undermined by the different ways jobs must be submitted to different machines. Obstacles to such a development arise from the difficulty of giving widely differing systems the same external interface (Dakin, 1975).

As far as our paper operating system is concerned we shall not attempt to design a particular job control language. Instead we simply remark that any job control language we adopt should contain the features described above, and be designed so as to incorporate those characteristics listed in section 11.2 as desirable from the user's point of view.


## 11.4 THE JOB POOL

We remarked in section 8.4 that jobs awaiting initiation by the scheduler are held in a *job pool*. Each entry in the job pool represents a single job, and contains information about it which is derived from the job description. This information is in fact an encoded form of that contained in the job description, except that in a spooling system all input device names are replaced by the names of the files into which the input has been spooled. The spooling may be performed by the job description interpreter itself, or the interpreter may delegate the task to separate input spoolers (see section 6.6) which it sets in motion by signalling the appropriate semaphores. In either case the interpreter signals to the scheduler whenever a new job pool entry is complete.

The job pool may be structured as a single list or as a number of lists each of which contains jobs with particular characteristics. The latter structure can be a help to the scheduler in choosing which job to run next.

The size of the job pool may prohibit its storage in main memory. However, storage on disc may involve the scheduler in heavy overheads when it comes to search for the best job to run. A possible compromise is to store abbreviated versions of the job pool entries in memory, while the complete entries reside on disc. The abbreviated entries will contain only such information as the scheduler needs to choose the next job; information about input files can, for example, be omitted.

## 11.5 SYSTEM MESSAGES

The relationship between the user and the operating system depends not only on how easily the user can tell the system what he wants it to do, but also on the quality of the information he receives from it about what it has done. The information supplied by current systems, particularly when job errors have occurred, varies widely in quantity, detail, relevance, and intelligibility. Ideally the degree of detail should depend on the fate of the job; if it terminates successfully then a brief account of the chargeable resources used is probably sufficient, but if it fails then a full statement of the cause is necessary. In all cases system messages should be couched in normal English in such a way as to be easily understood by a general user. All too frequently the user is presented with a mass of apparent gibberish, or, in the case of failure, with a hexadecimal dump!

In a multi-access environment a user should be able to request information about the current state of the system in terms of how many users are logged on, what resources are available, and so on. This information enables him to assess what kind of response he can expect and to decide whether or not it is worth while starting or continuing the session.

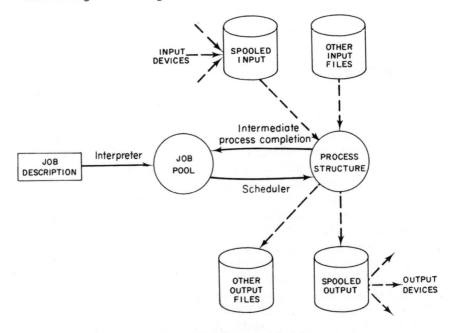

*Figure 11.5 Progress of a job*

## 11.6 PASSAGE OF A JOB THROUGH THE SYSTEM

Figure 11.5 summarises the stages by which a job progress from submission to termination through our paper operating system. The solid lines represent the various metamorphoses of the job from job description to job pool entry to sequence of processes; the broken lines represent the flow of data and programs associated with the job. If spooling is not employed then the input and output queues can be removed from the diagram and the data transfers shown as being direct to or from the peripheral devices. The circular motion between job pool and process structure is intended to emphasise that it may require the invocation of several processes to execute a single job. Within the process structure itself processes move between the three states blocked, runnable, and running, as previously shown in figure 8.4.

# Conclusion

In the last chapter we completed the construction of our paper operating system by providing it with an interface with the outside world. We also gave an overview of the system by describing the progress of a job from start to finish. It is probably appropriate at this stage to stand back a little and examine what we have achieved.

The purpose of building and describing the paper operating system has been twofold. The primary objective has been to use it as a vehicle for illustrating the mechanisms by which an operating system can fulfil the functions expected of it by its users. The secondary objective has been to support the increasingly popular view that operating systems can become reliable, easily maintained, and relatively error-free only if they exhibit a logically coherent structure. We shall return to this point in a moment.

As far as the primary aim is concerned it is hoped that the reader who has reached this point will have a good idea of what operating systems are, what they do, and how they do it. He should understand the nature of the problems posed in operating system design, and the techniques used for overcoming them. In a book as short as this it is of course impossible to give a comprehensive catalogue of all the problems and all the solutions; all one can do is describe those most frequently encountered or adopted. There will inevitably be systems which, because of different user environments or hardware constraints, present problems not covered here; similarly, there will be many systems in which the problems we have mentioned are solved in different ways. However, it is hoped that the material we have presented will provide an adequate basis from which the reader can broaden his knowledge according to his interests. The ground should be sufficiently well prepared for seeds from elsewhere to flourish.

The second point mentioned above, concerning the logical structure of operating systems, is one which merits further discussion. We have constructed on paper a system which is neatly layered, with each layer dependent only on the layers below it. However, it must be admitted that when we constructed the system the dice were loaded in our favour. First, we were not distracted by the problems of working in a large team, and second, we were not obliged by customer demand to add new features after the initial design stage. Third, and perhaps most important, we did not have to make the system work on a real machine. The question must therefore be asked: how far is it possible to translate the structure of the paper system into real life?

The first two obstacles – those of large project teams and changing specifications – can be avoided by judicious management. The third obstacle – that of intransigent machine architecture – is more difficult to overcome, particularly in the short term. Machine architecture impinges on the system at many levels, but the areas most directly influenced are interrupt handling, I/O, and memory protection. It is worth looking at each of these in turn.

As indicated in chapter 4, the complexity of the interrupt handler can vary greatly according to the amount of help given by the hardware. This help is particularly important in interrupt identification and in the determination of priorities. For example the DEC System-10, which provides a hardware priority interrupt mechanism in which devices may be assigned to any one of seven levels, gives more help than the IBM 370, in which priority is largely predetermined and can be modified only partially by selective software masking. Both machines do however provide adequate information for the source and nature of an interrupt to be readily determined.

The framework for I/O handling established in chapter 6 can become severely distorted by the constraints of a particular I/O architecture. The framework is well suited to architectures based on a simple bus system, but may have to be modified in cases (such as the IBM 370) involving a hierarchy of channels, control units, and devices. In the large CDC machines I/O functions are distributed among special peripheral processors, and the device handlers are executed by the peripheral processors rather than by a CPU. Teletypes, because of their special control function, are treated as special cases in most systems. On the DEC System-10, for example, teletype buffers are allocated from space belonging to the operating system, rather than (as is the case for other devices) from space belonging to individual user processes. The reason for this stems from the fact that a process which is performing I/O cannot be swapped out of main memory as its buffers might be overwritten. Since teletype buffers are always potentially in use it follows that if they were allocated from user space the corresponding user processes could never be swapped out.

The architectural feature which most seriously affects the structure of an operating system is probably the mechanism for memory protection. The total realisation of the layered structure of our paper operating system implies the existence of a protection system that can be made to mirror it. It seems that the segment, being the logical unit of address space, should be the natural unit for protection, and that what is required is the ability to create an arbitrary number of protection domains. One machine which departs far from the ideal is the IBM 370. Here protection is applied not to segments but to 2K byte blocks of physical memory; the confusion between logical and physical divisions of memory is made even worse by allowing the page field of an address to overflow into the segment field. Several machines, including the Burroughs 6700 and the Honeywell 645 apply protection to segments, but very few have more than two or three protection domains. The most common arrangement is the two-domain 'supervisor–user' system, typified by the IBM 370 and the ICL 1900. Multiple domains exist in the Honeywell 645 (MULTICS) system and the ICL 2900 series, but there are only a fixed number and they carry a high operational overhead. The problems of implementing multiple domains at low cost are by no means yet solved; the use of capabilities as described in chapter 9 is perhaps the most promising approach. However, despite the deficiencies of current architectures, we can expect that new protection mechanisms will soon provide the means for facilitating layered system structure. In the meantime we can regard structure as a legitimate objective while lacking the means to enforce it.

What other developments can be expected? Crystal ball gazing is a hazardous occupation in such a rapidly changing field, but we shall indulge in it briefly at the risk of being proved wrong by events. Short term developments are likely to be concentrated on improving the reliability of operating systems, on making them more easily portable between different machines, and on making them easier to use by means of more powerful and flexible job control languages. In the longer term the two factors we consider will most influence the nature and role of operating systems are the advent of microprocessors and the provision of improved telecommunications facilities.

Microprocessors offer a new form of processing power — small, discrete units of very low cost, in contrast to the large, monolithic, expensive units of the last 30 years. The challenge presented by microprocessors is to exploit this power to best advantage. One trend is already apparent: the dispersal of computing facilities to the places they are most needed, rather than their concentration in a central location. The rapidly decreasing cost of processors, memory, and secondary storage devices, has made it economically feasible to dedicate a complete computing system to a single application, be it payroll, process control, teaching, home budgeting, or whatever. Resource allocation, which is one of the chief functions of the traditional mainframe operating system, becomes trivial in such a dedicated system, since the resources required are always available.

Dedicated systems may be completely independent, or they may be linked by means of data transmission lines. In the latter case, information stored at one site can be transmitted for use at another, or work which is beyond the capacity of a single installation can be passed elsewhere for processing. The ability to link semi-independent installations into a large network gives the potential of delivering enormous computing power and information accessing capability to widely dispersed individuals or groups. The function of an operating system in such an environment includes message transmission and validation, load sharing, and the maintenance of the consistency of information which may be held in several forms at different sites.

Another possible development, in areas where large amounts of concentrated computing power are still required, is to replace the mainframe CPU by a collection of interconnected microprocessors. One advantage of doing this is that each process can have its own processor, thus increasing the parallelism in the system and eliminating the need for process switching. Another advantage is the potential increase in reliability which comes from the replication of processors. There are, however, several problems which must be overcome before such a system can be realised. One of the principal ones concerns memory organisation:

should each processor have its own private memory, should they all share a common memory, or should there be a combination of the two? Common memory brings problems of contention for access, while private memories imply a requirement for easy transmission of data between them. Mixed memory requires solutions to both types of problem, as well as that of devising and implementing an appropriate address map. Other architectural problems are the direction of external interrupts to the appropriate processor, and the provision of a mechanism for communication between processors. At the operating system level there are problems concerned with the recognition of potential parallelism, the allocation of processes to processors, communication between processes which may share no common memory, the sharing of resources, and error detection and recovery. All these problems are being vigorously tackled, and one can expect viable multi-microprocessor systems to become a reality within the next few years.

Finally, I would urge the reader not to regard this book as in any way a definitive study of operating systems. There are many excellent papers and books which will give fresh insight to the material covered here, or which will introduce the reader to new ground. It is hoped that the references given on the following pages will provide an adequate starting point.

# References

Alagic, S., and Arbib, M.A. (1978), *The Design of Well-Structured and Correct Programs*, Springer-Verlag, New York

Avizienis, A. (1977), Fault-tolerant Computing: Progress, Problems and Prospects, *Proceedings IFIPS 77*, North-Holland, Amsterdam, p. 405

Brooks, F.P. (1975), *The Mythical Man-Month*, Addison-Wesley, Reading, Mass.

Campbell, R.H., and Habermann, A.N. (1974), The specification of process synchronisation by path expressions, in *Lecture Notes in Computer Science*, **16**, Springer-Verlag, New York

Coffman, E.G., and Denning, P.J. (1973), *Operating System Theory*, Prentice-Hall, Englewood Cliffs, N.J.

Coffman, E.G., Elphick, M. and Shoshani, A. (1971), System deadlocks, *Computing Surveys*, **3**, 67-78

Coffman, E.G. and Kleinrock, L. (1968), Computer scheduling methods and their countermeasures, *Proceedings AFIPS Spring Joint Computer Conference*, **32**, 11-21

Colin, A.J.T. (1971), *Introduction to Operating Systems*, MacDonald-Elsevier, London and New York, p. 36

Corbató, F.J., Merwin-Dagget, M. and Daley, R.C. (1962), An experimental time sharing system, *Proceedings AFIPS Spring Joint Computer Conference*, **21**, 335-44

Courtois, P.J., Heymans, R. and Parnas, D.L. (1971), Concurrent control with "readers" and "writers", *Comm. ACM*, **14**, 667-8

Dahl, O.J., Dijkstra, E.W., and Hoare, C.A.R. (1972), *Structured Programming*, Academic Press, London and New York

Dakin, R.J. (1975), A general control language: structure and translation, *Computer Journal*, **18**, 324-32

Daley, R.C. and Dennis, J.B. (1968), Virtual memory, processes, and sharing in MULTICS, *Comm. ACM*, **11**, 306-12

Daley, R.C. and Neumann, P.G. (1965), A general-purpose file system for secondary storage, *Proceedings AFIPS Fall Joint Computer Conference*, **27**, 213-29

Denning, P.J. (1968), The working set model for program behaviour, *Comm. ACM*, **11**, 323-33

Denning, P.J. (1970), Virtual memory, *Computing Surveys*, **2**, 153-89

Denning, P.J. (1971), Third generation computer systems, *Computing Surveys*, **3**, 175-216

Denning, P.J. (1976), Fault-tolerant operating systems, *Computing Surveys*, **8**, 359–89

Dennis, J.B. and Van Horn, C. (1966), Programming semantics for multi-programmed computations, *Comm. ACM*, **9**, 143-55

Digital Equipment Corporation (1973), *DEC System-10 Assembly Language Handbook*, 3rd edition

Dijkstra, E.W. (1965), Cooperating sequential processes, In *Programming Languages* (ed. F. Genuys), Academic Press, New York, (1968)

Dijkstra, E.W. (1968), The structure of the T.H.E. multiprogramming system, *Comm. ACM*, **11**, 341-6

Dijkstra, E.W. (1976), *A Discipline of Programming*, Prentice-Hall, Englewood Cliffs, N.J.

England, D.M. (1974), The capability concept mechanism and structure in System-250, *IRIA International Workshop on Protection in Operating Systems*, Rocquencourt, 63–82

Evans, D.C. and Leclerc, J.Y. (1967), Address mapping and the control of access in an interactive computer, *Proceedings AFIPS Spring Joint Computer Conference*, **30**, 23-32

Fabry, R.S. (1974), Capability based addressing, *Comm. ACM*, **17**, 403–12

Floyd, R.W. (1967), Assigning meanings to programs, *Proc. Symposium in Applied Maths*, **19**, American Math. Soc.

Foster, C.C. (1970), *Computer Architecture*, Van Nostrand Reinhold, New York, pp. 146-52

Frank, G.R. (1976), Job control in the MU5 operating system, *Computer Journal*, **19**, 139–43

Fraser, A.G. (1969), Integrity of a mass storage filing system, *Computer Journal*, **12**, 1-5

Graham, G.S. and Denning, P.J. (1972), Protection – principles and practice, *Proceedings AFIPS Spring Joint Computer Conference*, **40**, 417-29

Graham, R.M. (1968), Protection in an information processing utility, *Comm. ACM*, **11**, 365-9

Habermann, A.N. (1969), Prevention of system deadlock, *Comm. ACM*, **12**, 373-7

Habermann, A.N. (1972), Synchronisation of communicating processes, *Comm. ACM*, **15**, 171-6

Hansen, P.B. (1970), The nucleus of a multiprogramming system, *Comm. ACM*, **13**, 238-50

Hansen, P.B. (1972), Structured multiprogramming, *Comm. ACM*, **15**, 574-8

Hansen, P.B. (1973), *Operating System Principles*, Prentice-Hall, Englewood Cliffs, N. J.

Hansen, P.B. (1975), The programming language Concurrent Pascal, *IEEE Trans. Software Engineering*, **1**, 199–207

Hansen, P.B. (1978), Distributed processes: a concurrent processing concept, *Comm. ACM*, **21**, 934–941

Hantler, S.L., and King, J.C. (1976), An introduction to proving the correctness of programs, *Computing Surveys*, **8**, 331–53

Hartley, D.F. (1970), Management software in multiple-access systems, *Bulletin of the I.M.A.*, **6**, 11–13

Havender, J.W. (1968), Avoiding deadlock in multitasking systems, *IBM Systems Journal*, **7**, 74–84

Hoare, C.A.R. (1972), Proof of correctness of data representation, *Acta Informatica*, **1**, 271–81

Hoare, C.A.R. (1974), Monitors: an operating system structuring concept, *Comm. ACM*, **17**, 549–57

Horning, J., Lauer, H.C., Melliar-Smith, P.M., and Randell, B. (1974), A program structure for error detection and recovery, in *Lecture Notes in Computer Science*, **16**, Springer-Verlag, New York

Huxtable, D.H.R., and Pinkerton, J.M.M. (1977), The hardware/software interface of the ICL 2900 range of computers, *Computer Journal*, **20**, 290–5

IBM Corporation, *IBM System 360/ Operating System Concepts and Facilities*, Manual C28-6535

ICL (1969), *Operating Systems George 3 and 4*, Manual 4169

IFIP (1969), *File Organisation,* Selected papers from File 68, IFIP Administrative Data Processing Group, occasional publication number 3, Swets and Zeitliger

Jackson, M. (1975), *Principles of Program Design*, Academic Press, London and New York

Judd, D.R. (1973), *Use of Files*, MacDonald-Elsevier, London and New York

Keedy, J.L. (1976), The management and technological approach to the design of System B, *Proc. 7th Australian Computer Conf.*, Perth, 997–1013

Knuth, D.E. (1968), *The Art of Computer Programming*, vol. 1 Fundamental algorithms, Addison-Wesley, Reading, Mass.

Kopetz, H. (1979), *Software Reliability*, Macmillan, London and Basingstoke

Lister, A.M. (1974), Validation of systems of parallel processes, *Computer Journal*, **17**, 148–51

Martin, J. (1977), *Computer Data-Base Organisation*, 2nd ed., Prentice-Hall, Englewood Cliffs, N.J.

Randell, B. (1975), System structure for software fault tolerance, *IEEE Trans. Software Engineering*, **1**, 220–32

Randell, B., Lee, P.A., and Treleaven, P.C. (1978), Reliability issues in computing system design, *Computing Surveys*, **10**, 123–65

Richards, M. (1969), BCPL: a tool for compiler writing and systems programming. *Proceedings AFIPS Spring Joint Computer Conference*, **34**, 557–66

Ritchie, D.M., and Thompson, K. (1974), The UNIX time-sharing system, *Comm. ACM*, **17**, 365–75

Schroeder, M.D. and Saltzer, J.H. (1972), A hardware architecture for implementing protection rings, *Comm. ACM*, **15**, 157–70

Stone, H.S. (ed.) (1975), *An Introduction to Computer Architecture*, SRA, Chicago

Svobodova, L. (1976), *Computer Performance Measurement and Evaluation*, Elsevier, New York

Watson, R.W. (1970), *Timesharing System Design Concepts*, McGraw-Hill, New York

Williams, R.K. (1972), System 250 – basic concepts. *Proceedings of the Conference on Computers – Systems and Technology*, I.E.R.E. Conference Proceedings number 25, 157–68

Wirth, N. (1971), Program development by stepwise refinement, *Comm. ACM*, **14**, 221–7

Wirth, N. (1977), Modula: a language for modular multiprogramming, *Software Practice and Experience*, **7**, 3–36

Wulf, W.A. (1975), Reliable hardware-software architecture, *IEEE Trans. Software Engineering*, **1**, 233–40

Wulf, W.A., Russell, D.B. and Habermann, A.N. (1971), BLISS: a language for systems programming, *Comm. ACM*, **14**, 780–90

Yourdon, E. (1975), *Techniques of Program Structure and Design*, Prentice-Hall, Englewood Cliffs, N.J.

# Index